Praise for *Nature's Housekeeper*

"Thoreau meets Hunter S. Thompson in *Nature's Housekeeper*, Michael Gurnow's witty addition to the naturalist shelf. Get ready to giggle, guffaw, and LOL all over your new Timberlands: *Nature's Housekeeper* follows one man's morph from hapless Ranger Ned into sly Deerslayer, from a wasp-, nettle-, and pride-stung rube into a mind skinny dipping in the green outlands. And just like that Transcendentalist blue-jay Thoreau, Gurnow teaches you a D.I.Y. survival trick or three while making you laugh your copperheads off."

> ~ Ron Dakron, author of *Hello Devilfish!*

"Laughing my survival a## off page-by-page, Gurnow's *Nature's Housekeeper* made me want to go live and work in the woods . . . oh wait a minute, that's what I do!"

> ~ Survivorman Les Stroud

"*Nature's Housekeeper* pulls off the difficult and unique feat of marrying comedy, wilderness philosophy, and practical trail work into one entertaining and informative whole. Packed with humorous incidents, stories, and comments, the book had me laughing out loud, yet at the same time the central tale of how a virulently anti-nature, city-loving college professor overcomes his loathing of wild places through reading Thoreau (backed up later by Annie Dillard and Aldo Leopold) and, 1960s style, drops out of academia to become a trail maintenance worker is moving and intellectually profound. Beyond the comedy there is great depth here and much to ponder."

> ~ Chris Townsend, author of the award-winning
> *The Backpacker's Handbook* and editor for *The Great
> Outdoors* magazine

"Gurnow's metamorphosis from urbanite to woodsman will leave you in stitches! *Nature's Housekeeper* entertains every step of the way and may even leave you with a burning desire to get outside – or at least a burning desire to get rid of that poison ivy rash."

> ~ Lawton Grinter, host of 'The Trail Show' and author of
> *I Hike*

"With his acclaimed wit and clarity, Michael Gurnow synthesizes academic disciplines to awaken the reader, forcing his audience to reconsider two crucial areas — Nature (brutalized by us) and materialism (which brutalizes us). Read, rethink, change and 'regain paradise!'"

> ~ Betty F. Cooper, Ph.D.; educator, activist, facilitator, dopeace.us.

"Michael Gurnow gives us a laugh-out-loud, page-turning memoir with *Nature's Housekeeper* and proof that a physical return to the outdoors can provide simplicity and fulfillment. This is a must-read for anyone looking to reconnect with nature or hoping to see wilderness through a different lens."

> ~ Jennifer Pharr Davis, author of *Becoming Odyssa*

"This is the power of Gurnow's *Nature's Housekeeper*: It uses humor to communicate, in subtle ways at first, and more poignantly at the end, the why, where, and how of developing a deeper and richer understanding of humanity's role in becoming better stewards of the Earth. And that is definitely worth a read!"

> ~ Buddy Huffaker, President & Executive Director, The Aldo Leopold Foundation

"Reading *Nature's Housekeeper* is like sitting around the table sharing drinks and laughing with Thoreau, Herriot, Twain, Abbey, and Lenny Bruce. But be sure to wipe those laughter-sponsored tears from your eyes every once in a while because Gurnow's adventure is nothing short of a hero's journey that would make Joseph Campbell proud."

> ~Brian King, Founder & Director, Wilderness Skills Institute

"Michael Gurnow's eco-comedy *Nature's Housekeeper* made me think of the Cullinan. Not a single 540-carat diamond but rather 540 one-carat diamonds. A treasury of mind-expanding adventures, full of wisdom and sudden insights that will take you by surprise."

> ~Daniel Quinn, author of *Ishmael* and *The Story of B*

Nature's Housekeeper

An Eco-Comedy

Michael Gurnow

Blue River Press
Indianapolis, Indiana

Nature's Housekeeper
©2015 by Michael Gurnow

Published by Blue River Press
2402 N. Shadeland Avenue, Suite A
Indianapolis, Indiana 46219
www.brpressbooks.com

A Tom Doherty Company, Inc. imprint
Distributed by Cardinal Publishers Group
317-352-8200 phone
317-352-8202 fax
www.cardinalpub.com

ISBN: 978-1-935628-48-4

Cover Design: Kevin Essett
Edited by: Charleen Davis
Book design by: Dave Reed
Editorial assistance by Timothy Chism and Tom Gibbons
Printed in the United States of America

10 9 8 7 6 5 4 3 2 1

For my wife.

May you continue to enjoy the idea of nature.

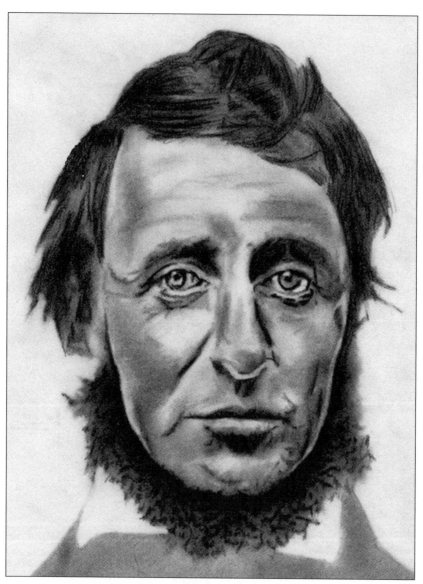

Henry David Thoreau

CONTENTS

Acknowledgements

Though written with the assistance of the Missouri State Park system, the organization—as it has with previous texts dealing with state-funded institutions—asked that I abstain from issuing *explicit* credit to express individuals or particular parks so as not to imply preferential treatment of one recreational center or employee over the next. Due to the fact that I discuss my experiences in several state parks, one of which I only visited once while having worked in another for seven years, I do not cite any by their formal titles and, to further veil the parks' identities, have changed their trail names as well. Fortunately for the reader, administration said nothing about divulging heavy-handed context clues . . .

As such, I would like to thank anyone who has, for better or worse, had the courage to step into the woods and those who make it possible for the gallant few to do so with the least amount of (un)due complication. The end result is that, regardless of the outcome, it almost always makes for a great story.

May your hiking and camping be horny hornet-free.

A Note to the Reader

Any first-year psychology student or fan of police procedurals knows an observed event is subject to perspective, the retelling of which is further fictionalized by the corruption of memory and personal bias. With that, although what follows is based on true events and actual people, narrative constraints obligated me to condense, omit, reorganize, hedge, and embellish the particulars on more than one occasion.

What you have in your hands is what I like to call a "less-than-fictional" autobiography of my time spent in nature. To be more accurate, it is a biography I've written about a guy that happens to have the same name and had many of the same experiences as the author and, rather suspiciously, is also married to my wife.

As these things tend to go, I have changed the names of those involved to protect the guilty and mock the innocent.

Also, following the tradition of nature writing and for the sake of brevity, I have elected to compress seven years of trail maintenance experience into four seasons. I hope they are as fun for the reader as they were for me, minus the nudity and bladder-voiding copperheads.

Introduction

Why Leopold, Why Gurnow?

"We can be ethical only in relation to something we can see, feel, understand, love, or otherwise have faith in."

— Aldo Leopold
A Sand County Almanac

If you are reading this book, you fall into one of three groups:

You already have a passion for, and deep sense of, responsibility to the natural world.

You are in the process of developing a passion for, and responsibility to, the natural world.

You don't have a passion for, and certainly not a responsibility to, the natural world. However, someone close to you, a friend or family member, desperately wishes you did.

Undoubtedly this doesn't cover everyone in the universe, but I am pretty confident that the aforementioned groups represent 99 percent of those who will be introduced to this book.

Hopefully those in Groups 1 and 2 will have some awareness of Aldo Leopold and his book *A Sand County Almanac*, which has informed and inspired readers around the world to care about — and for — the natural world. If you haven't heard of him, you will after reading *Nature's Housekeeper*. All books and other means of communication help provide us with a vocabulary to understand what we share in common, as well as our differences. Arguably, no book has done this better for how we view and value the natural world than Leopold's *A Sand County Almanac*. In this now classic volume, Leopold asks us to include the plants, animals, soil, water, and air in our definition of our community and extend to them the same kind of ethical considerations we give, or should give, our friends and family.

But as the quote at the beginning of this introduction demonstrates, Leopold recognizes that in order to *really* extend these considerations and values to our co-habitants on this planet, it requires us to have knowledge about, and interaction with, the wild world out there. And there is no better way to engage nature than to throw oneself into it, just as our protagonist does in *Nature's Housekeeper*. Gurnow shares the follies and foils of someone that wants to engage the wilds, but finds that they are, well, wild!

Nearly anyone that has attempted to hike, camp, fish, hunt, photograph, or otherwise spend time outdoors in a true wilderness area—or even a city park—can sympathize with finding themselves in over their head, hopefully only with trauma to their ego, but sometimes to their body and, at times, to key relationships in their lives. No matter where you are on this journey, this book helps remind us that the road to an ecological conscience is not always straight and fast; it often has zigs, zags, stings, and poison ivy.

So, if you are in Group 3 and aren't totally sure why someone you know has recommended or even given you a copy of this book, do take the time to read it. At a minimum, you will laugh and be introduced to Aldo Leopold and others that have shaped our American experience. And even if it doesn't compel you to change your life and dive headfirst into a career of trail maintenance, it will most certainly give you insights into the vision and values of your loved one.

If you are in Group 2 and are concerned that you are finding *way* too much in common with Gurnow's experiences, know that he not only survived, but found life more complete and fulfilling as a result of the pain and suffering. The old adage of "What doesn't kill you makes you stronger" rings true once again. But for readers in this group, pay particular attention to the end of the book where the daily struggles are given bigger and broader context. Too often we don't connect the particular with the profound. Small actions and big ideas must always be married together as we think about our place in the world and how we can make it better.

Finally, if you are in Group 1, I am guessing you are trying to decide which of your friends or relatives in Group 3 you want to give a copy of this book. There are of course many books you could share by luminaries such as Aldo Leopold, Henry David Thoreau, John Muir, Rachel Carson, Wendell Berry, etc. But one thing I think we should all have great faith in—but the conservation community seems all too often to neglect—is the power of humor.

This is the power of Gurnow's *Nature's Housekeeper*: It uses humor to communicate, in subtle ways at first, and more poignantly at the end, the why, where, and how of developing a deeper and richer understanding of humanity's role in becoming better stewards of the Earth. And *that* is definitely worth a read!

Buddy Huffaker
President & Executive Director
The Aldo Leopold Foundation
Baraboo, Wisconsin
September 2014

The Aldo Leopold Foundation is a 501(c)3 not-for-profit, donor-supported organization based at the Leopold Legacy Center in Baraboo, Wisconsin. The foundation's mission is to inspire an ethical relationship between people and the land. As the owner and caretaker of the original Aldo Leopold Shack, the organization works with public and private landowners to demonstrate how a Land Ethic can be used to guide stewardship and restoration activities on over 10,000 acres along the Wisconsin River. Furthermore, the foundation serves as the executor of Leopold's literary estate, encourages scholarship on his life and concept of a Land Ethic, and acts as a clearinghouse for information regarding the writer, his work, and his ideas. Education programs at the Leopold Center serve thousands of visitors from around the world and many thousands more are served through its website, the Green Fire *film about the author, and other outreach programming, including a database of Leopold teaching tools for educators.*

"As for conforming outwardly, and living your own life inwardly, I do not think much of that."

> — Henry David Thoreau
> Letter to Harrison Blake
> August 9, 1850

"He wears a mask, and his face grows to fit it."

> — George Orwell
> "Shooting an Elephant"

Preface

I have the worst job in the world. I'm not kidding. Ninety-nine percent of the people that get hired to do what I do don't bother showing up the next day. They don't even call.

I don't blame them. If I were them, I'd leave dirty messages on the answering machine.

Let me explain.

When someone gets hired on, they are expected to work in all conceivable weather conditions, have no job security, and by merely clocking in, run the risk of never seeing home again—seriously. These poor souls don't even have access to running water or a bathroom during the workday. Benefits? P-shaw! Promotion opportunities, sma-motion opportunities. Equipment? Well, yes, it's graciously provided, but employees must keep it on them at all times. It only weighs 30 to 75 pounds. Oh, did I mention new hires must walk—not drive—*walk* several miles each and every day before they can start to do anything remotely productive?

I know what you're thinking. This is why we get paid the big bucks, right?

I make minimum wage.

What is this God-awful job I have that no one else can stand?

My friends, I am a trail maintenance worker.

And I wouldn't trade it for the world.

Though people often laugh when I tell them this, if I were offered a six-figure salary complete with benefits, bonuses, a private bathroom, and company car, I'd turn around and go right back into the woods.

I've found that people are kind of funny this way. I've met a few who seem rather fond of money, climate control, and being able to wash their hands whenever the mood strikes. It's been my experience that these are the same individuals who like their odds of lounging in their favorite recliner ever again to be fairly good.

But I ask you, *Where's the fun in that?*

I'm not championing the cause because I'm trying to hide a handful of sour grapes. No, no. It's not that I *can't* have a white-collar career. I did. I've got a stack of college degrees. I held a salaried position. I had my own desk, health insurance, and easy access to toiletries.

I know what you're thinking.

No, I didn't get fired. I didn't get laid off. I quit.

I quit because I was going insane. I'd lost myself. I had no clue who the stunningly good-looking guy was that kept staring back at me when I looked in the mirror. I wanted, needed something completely different.

And that is what I got — and get — every day when I go to work.

I eat lunch 220 feet in the air or on the banks of one of the mightiest rivers in the world.

I don't have to manage employees, review budgets, deal with customers, file paperwork, or meet with clients.

I work in a place where people wait to go on vacation, which just so happens to be one of the most popular getaways in America: In 2013, Missouri was voted Best Trail State in the nation and, later that year, a statewide poll rated my park *Numero Uno.*

I get to see things on a daily basis which, when others see them for the first time, changes their lives forever. It continues to change mine every day too.

So how'd I go from white-collar to brown-collar? Well, it's a bit more complicated than me just deciding to take a proverbial walk in the park one lazy afternoon. What you have in your hands is the story of how I went from being a nerdy college student to a guy who had no business traipsing off into the woods and almost died there, all before becoming the strapping individual made better for giving nature a second, third, and fourth chance. (Literally.)

I'll be the first to admit it wasn't always easy and it wasn't always enjoyable, but it's always funny in retrospect. In the end, I'd like to say I found myself but, alas, every day I enter the forest I discover something about me, and life, that I didn't know before.

How many people can say that about their job?

I wholeheartedly recommend everyone to do the same. I don't mean throw caution to the wind and become a TMW but, rather, get a taste of the good life: Take a hike; get a little nature on you. But before you do, thumb through this quaint little tale so you know why it's frowned upon to be caught naked in the woods, what to do when a deer tries to take your life, and how to spot the elusive tree snorer.

Enjoy.

Michael Gurnow
Oriole, Missouri
December 2014

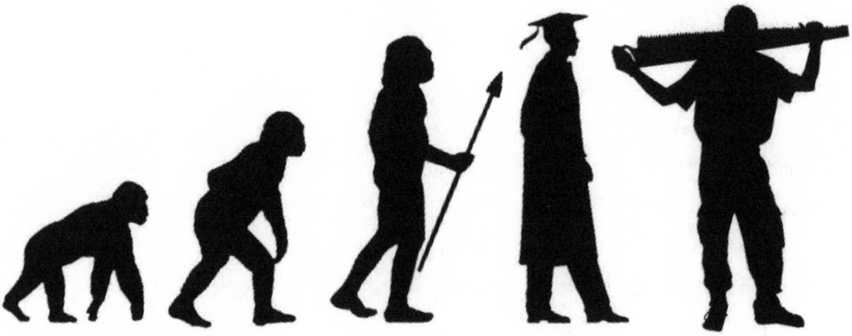

Nature's Housekeeper

Chapter 1

The Unsuspecting Taxi Driver

How bad could it be? I now understood that many a premature death was prefaced by this simple, naïve, rhetorical question.

It was my first semester as a graduate student in American literature and I had recently met a small, dark-haired, introverted female of uncertain genealogical descent. An uneasy relationship at best, she was much more comfortable around her friends than with me. As a result, I often found myself on dates with her and a handful of her compatriots. Desperate to make the relationship work, I reluctantly agreed to transport her to where her pals would be spending their free time over the course of a weekend, a state park approximately two hours away.

How bad could it be? This coming from the only child of Baby Boomers who devoutly believed in the byline that technology would be humanity's savior. As such, I had never been camping. Though barely out of my teens, I had never set foot on a nature trail. I didn't know how to swim. My professionally aloof girlfriend planned to do two out of three of these activities with her friends over the next couple of days.

How bad could it be? I asked myself. Despite her introversion, my girlfriend could have run for mayor. Even though each and every time I went out with her, her friends were involved in some capacity, I never met the same person twice. I quietly suspected she might have been using me solely because her social circle was so large, her buddies never had room for her in the car. I wasn't her boyfriend; I was her cabbie. But because I had dated quite extensively after starting college, her popularity created the perfect conditions for a probability shit storm.

How bad could it be? Oh silly, silly man.

After a two-hour drive which seemed like six, as the radio kept me company although my significant other sat mere inches away, we arrived at the campsite. Her friends were already there. Day-Glo orange, lime green, and battleship gray tents littered the surrounding area like an improvised settlement. Some of the males were already bringing firewood back from the woodshed as the girls busily set out food on a nearby picnic table. As we approached, I heard an ominous, "Oh God."

By the time I aligned the source of the utterance with the utterer, I only caught a fleeting glimpse of a female's back. She already had another girl's bicep firmly in her grasp and was hurriedly dragging the individual in the opposite direction. As I sidled up to the boys and introduced myself, my girlfriend darted off in the direction the two females had fled. Before I had the chance to feign outdoor male conversation by gruffly asking if anyone had gotten a deer that season and nonchalantly turning my head and spitting, I noticed a trio of figures marching toward us. Few things in this world evoke testicle-shriveling fear in a man like a group of frowning women, enraged to the point of atypical silence, ambling toward him with an obvious agenda. I looked up and instinctively mumbled under my breath, "Oh God."

There stood my reticent girlfriend, a person whom I did not know, and my blonde ex-girlfriend. This might not have been a problem if it weren't for the fact I'd cheated on the latter two months prior. Par for a mind trained in the literature classroom, I remember thinking to myself that this couldn't be a good sign: Both the light and dark sides were conspiring against me as I became the caldron the Macbethian witches were about to light a match under. I only had time to make a mental note to start hitting on redheads before the shouted reprimands and "How could you's?" started pummeling at me. Even the girl that I didn't know, had no association with, and who had never laid eyes on me charitably contributed to my ass-chewing. What I learned in the process was that both of my ex-girlfriends (I readily assumed I was now relieved of boyfriend/taxi driver duty) were terrific individuals who deserved better; I was a despicable, disgusting, dreadful, deplorable person along with another word that begins with the letter D; and toward the end of the joint diatribe, advised to challenge the laws of physics and human anatomy.

A rational person would have left and, indeed, I believed myself to fall under this heading because, alas, although I was on my way to becoming a literature scholar, I was already a philosopher. At least that's what my undergraduate diploma said. However, there was a problem. This rational thinker has a horrible sense of direction and had no clue where he was. A stereotypical male, my mental physiology prohibited my mouth from being able to form the words which, in response, garners directions. I was stuck.

I went on to learn a lot about nature that weekend, starting the first night. For example, though late summer, it gets alarmingly cold in the woods after sundown and, without a roof over your head, your shirt can gather a remarkable amount of bone-chilling dew by the time dawn breaks. I discovered that staring into a bonfire that you yourself have made has its rewards — not because you were forced to get the wood, light it, and keep it going all night long in order to stave off hypothermia because those whom you are sharing a campsite made it abundantly clear their nice, warm, already burning inferno wasn't for you — but rather its dancing flames does a fair job of keeping your mind off the famine-inducing hunger you are experiencing because your now ex-girlfriend's friends refuse to share their food.

After the sun opted to take pity on me and broke the horizon, I sat at the predetermined distance the camp had decided was permissible to keep a leper and watched as everyone ate a big, full, piping-hot breakfast before preparing to go for a swim. Tired of shivering in front of my own personal campsite and having nothing better to do, I followed everyone into the park like an abused, abandoned, cow-eyed puppy. My lessons in nature quickly resumed.

I soon learned there are three prerequisites to a decent existence: sleep, food, and the often overlooked creature comfort known as thermal regulation. Because I had none of these, a Saharan sun set upon me like two-and-a-half very ticked off ex-girlfriends. After

3

watching the well-rested and fed swimmers of the world who were undoubtedly running temperatures that could be recorded on a standard thermometer, I decided to try my best impression of self-respect.

I had noticed a sign designating the start of a trail a little ways from where everyone was cooling themselves in the water. Its entrance, littered with friendly pebbles amid calf-high grasses which were gently billowing in the morning breeze, looked inviting enough. If nothing else, I could temporarily escape the death glares which were being cast in my direction at regular intervals. At worst, my entourage would leave without me. If worst came to worse, I'd buy a map. I could see the walkway ambled into a grove of trees which cast sunstroke-inhibiting shadows. When I heard passersby casually mention the trail which lay before me was the longest in the park, a scant 10 miles, I thought to myself I could at least say I accomplished something on this particular weekend other than getting dumped. I entered the welcoming pathway without saying a word to anyone.

It was a miracle I was ever heard from again.

At the beginning, the trail kept its genteel promise. It ran along a clichéd babbling brook before gradually easing away from those who had rejected me. Almost imperceptibly, the pebbles became sand. By the time my feet met solid ground once more, the threat of heatstroke exponentially plummeted because I had finally made it to the edge of the woods. To my relief, no human noise could be heard. My morale began to return. I passed from one ecosystem to the next. Happy little clouds watched over me as I made my way through calming, Elysian grasslands which leisurely metamorphosed into fields of massive, delicate ferns. Ferns gave way to contented shrubbery. Shrubbery transformed into amiable, broadleaf, waist-high foliage that waved to me with each cooling zephyr. By this time, eager saplings had become proud, respectable trees. I realized I was in a forest. Just as I noticed the first signs of fatigue, the terrain's slope increased in severity. I gallantly pressed onward and upward.

The respectable trees started to become indifferent columns of wood, which quickly surrendered to dominating, vindictive sentries of the forest. Regardless of how many hills I crested, another malevolently awaited me on the other side. Once mental frustration sat in, I sped up. I was ready to be off the trail. When my thirst became unbearable (I hadn't seen a need to bring water since driving 10 miles only took approximately eight minutes), I began to lightly sprint. I knew the average human walked at a rate of three or four miles an hour; we run at around six. I estimated I had been on the trail a few hours already, so I reasoned that the end must be near, especially since I was now traveling at least five miles per hour. It then occurred to me that the slapping I was hearing was the sloppy sound of my shoes on granite. I had to shake off my inability to recall when the terrain had changed without my noticing. The malicious hills promptly morphed into crag-filled mountains. Then something horrible happened.

Right after I started sprinting, either my hyperactive, frantic movement; the smell of desperation tinged with panic; or my blaring gullibility piqued the interest of a hornet with a case of mistaken identity: It believed itself to be a fighter jet. I waved my hands in the air, trying to shoo it away. It persisted. Its concentric surveys of me became more frequent and aggressive as it tightened its perimeter. I moved to a dead run. The hornet pursued. I took off my shirt and begun swinging it over my head. The black-and-yellow insect that so desperately needed to sting me apparently mistook this as an invitation to a fight, or rough hornet sex. I was not so much worried about its motive as I was its intent. I started screaming.

I vaguely remember passing some fool crouched down in front of a boulder. Apparently no one had informed him that the Apocalypse had arrived. Instead of plagues of locusts, a single hornet was sent to finish off humanity, starting with me. I assumed the individual was taking moss samples: He had tweezers in one hand and a plastic vial in the other. Upon hearing the approaching one-man stampede, he turned to look over his shoulder. The sudden appearance of a screaming, rabid, sleep-deprived, famished, dehydrated, half-naked bookworm twirling his t-shirt over his head as if he were at a football rally left him stupefied.

All he was able to manage at the sight of what I could only guess was a fairly regular occurrence for anyone insane enough to go hiking was to pivot on the balls of his feet and watch as I ran past. He didn't utter so much as a kindly, "Do you need help?" I prayed that once the hornet had finished with me, it'd immediately return for the moss collector.

Then, without rhyme or reason, God decided to postpone humanity's end. All of a sudden, not unlike the climax of many a bad horror film, the dark vaginal tunnel of the forest cast me out. The wicked, evil wilds had spat me onto a freshly hewed lawn. Families at picnic tables turned to look at me as I, doubled-over and heaving, tried to catch my breath. To my left sat the visitor center. Stunned that a world existed outside the Sisyphean woods, only then did I become aware that the mad hornet was gone. Perhaps it was the warden of the woods and I had reached the edge of its dictatorial domain. Maybe it had been a winged Cerberus guarding the gates of overgrown, green hell. It wouldn't have surprised me if it was the Devil incarnate. I no longer cared. I was simply glad it was gone.

The next thing I knew I was in the air-conditioned visitor center. My shirt had somehow been put back on me. I was standing in front of the cashier's desk. Five glistening, life-giving ambrosial bottles of water sat before me on the counter as my now sweat-drenched wallet wilted in my right hand. I was obligated to look at the total on the cash register's screen because when the clerk told me how much I owed her, her voice was a faint, indiscernible echo far, far away. I paid, found a table, and proceeded to inhale three of the bottles. I paused to relish and give thanks for the fourth. I kept the fifth in case the forest began encroaching.

After gaining a glimpse of heaven, like a coma victim, I slowly accepted my moral obligation to return to the mortal world. As if cruelly timed, just as I pushed open the door leading back into the park, my ex-girlfriend and her barrage of me-hating friends came up from the campsite. She begrudgingly walked up to me and said it was time to leave. I naively let myself utter a sigh of relief, thinking the worst weekend of my life had come to a close. She then informed me there was no room in her friend's car and that I would be driving her home.

Whereas I had been serenaded by the radio on our way to the park, my ex-girlfriend spent the entire two-hour trip back without so much as pausing to take a breath. I was almost relieved when I got a flat. I had a legitimate excuse to get away from her for a few minutes. It must have been an entertaining sight for those traveling along the interstate to witness a small brunette berating a man, replete with a wagging finger in his face, as he changed a tire in the midday sun. Mobile once more, approximately three-quarters of the way home I mindlessly reached down to scratch my calf. As I did so, my finger ran over a bump. As I grabbed fold upon fold of pant leg, pulling upward with each handful, I divided my attention between the road and my calf. I temporarily lost control of the vehicle when I finally got a good look at the protrusion. It was a tick.

I had never had a tick before, much less one imbedded in me. I remembered from grade school there was a right way and a wrong way to remove a tick. I dared not attempt delicate tick-removal surgery upon myself while driving, lest I chance breaking off the head which would inevitably become infected, gangrenous, and end with the loss of my favorite leg, if not the whole lower half of my body, of which I had also grown quite fond over the years. Fearful she would deliberately botch the procedure and then force-feed me the bug, I abstained from asking my ex-girlfriend for assistance. This matter demanded my complete, undivided, and well-rested and fed attention. It would have to wait until I got home. For the remaining half hour of my time on the road with her, I didn't hear a word my ex-girlfriend all but screamed. My mind was busy running through the various medical complications that could ensue from a tick bite. I tried to remember their names and symptoms: Lyme disease, Rocky Mountain spotted fever, ehrlichiosis, tularemia, and youregoingtodieosis leapt to mind.

To my utter amazement, I made it safely home, severed ties with my girlfriend, and extracted the tick without undue complication. As I tossed my entomological souvenir from the forest in the trash, I noticed a slight twinge on the big toe of my left foot. I took off my sock and pressed down on the nail. White puss shot out. On top of it all, I had managed to get my first ingrown toenail. To make matters worse, the week before, my girlfriend of a day prior had painted my toenails while I was asleep. For the average person, this wouldn't be a problem anymore than driving out of a state park after asking for directions. But I was one of the lucky few who suffered from podophobia, a fear of feet. My psychological handicap was so severe I had serious issues with my own tootsies. Draining the wound had been nothing short of a Herculean effort. Removing the nail polish was out of the question. My ex-girlfriend undoubtedly continued to laugh at my expense the next day as I took off my sock and graced the doctor with a dancing rainbow of color. He received my explanation in much the same manner as the sales associate who is told the *Playboy* you are buying is for a friend.

An understandable badge of honor, I went on to tell the tale of having hiked the longest pathway in the park for many, many proud years. A decade later, as I relayed my travails to a veteran hiker of the region, I was interrupted mid-story.

"Mike, you sure you've got the right trail?"

Slightly offended at the implication his question suggested, I responded, "Without a doubt. Why?"

"Well," he opened with a reluctant pause of hesitation, almost always indicative of bad news, "it doesn't sound like you were on Crowder."

Daunted, I looked at him.

He continued, "Crowder's the 10-mile trail. From the way you're talking, you were on one of the shorter ones. If I had to guess, I'd say you'd hiked the Tourist Trail."

I didn't like what I was hearing and I *definitely* didn't care for the insinuation that went along with having traveled the length of a footpath dubbed the "Tourist Trail." This implied that I might have had trouble with a route designed for overweight retirees, asthmatic children, and arthritic senior citizens. But it was clear he knew what he was talking about and, worse yet, he'd spoken that glory-depriving word, "shorter."

I grudgingly asked, "How long are the other trails out there?"

He placed one hand on his hip as the other met his lip while he paused to consider.

"Well, they're all about two miles, give or take, unless . . ."

I stood a bit more erect at the sheer possibility.

". . . you did the Mountain section all in one day."

I saw my chance for ego redemption and took it.

"How long's that one?"

"Thirty-five," he replied with a wry smile.

Although my descent into hell seemed to have gone on forever, I knew it wasn't possible for me to have hiked 35 miles that day. To add insult to injury, I also realized that even if I had traversed 10 miles, I hadn't even completed the longest in the park. My stature as a trail deity was automatically downgraded to demigod and was on the brink of being relegated to mere mortal. Having already exhibited denial and anger at the death of my reputation, I quickly started bargaining.

"I know what it is," I assured him. "They probably—Oh, what's the word for it?—*amended* one of those you're talking about. That tourist one."

"No," he affirmed, "I don't think so; not to my knowledge. I've been on those trails since before you started high school. They've done some reroutes over the years, but they haven't had to close a section on any of them out there," he said, somewhat apologetically now that he saw how the hard, sadistic truth was affecting me.

Having heard little after "No," and what little trail jargon I did catch making almost no sense to me, I tried to wrap my mind around having been browbeaten by a scant two miles of nature walkway. With great aplomb which summarily closed the book on my legendary effort, he proceeded to reinforce his argument by describing the trail I had been on in exacting detail, so much so that I had micro flashbacks of my day touring Lucifer's Playground. After he was done, there was no doubt he was right. I had only hiked a couple of miles.

This was my introduction to nature. It was clear then that the wilderness was telling me I was an unwanted guest. I graciously took its advice and swore I would never enter another state park ever again.

Chapter 2

Fraggle Fern

I was back in another state park the following year. A high school friend had gotten a job as a trail maintenance worker at a park just a few miles from where we were attending college. He invited me to keep him company at work one afternoon. I shot back a steadfast "No." He insisted, assuring me a good time would be had by all. I adamantly protested, called him a no-good liar, and stated nature had already done its level best to place me in an early grave and I would be damned if I'd let it have another stab at me. He started to beg. I informed him I had evolved beyond sticks and twigs, that I was the fabled post-postmodern man, and my body had subsequently adapted to climate control and indoor plumbing. He nonetheless doggedly persisted over the course of the next several weeks.

Time and hubris are malevolent magicians. After selective amnesia had chinked away large chunks of the longest weekend of my life in order to protect my sanity, my ego did the rest of the talking. Aided by his incessant appeals, I gradually convinced myself that my previous brush with death at the hands of nature had, in fact, not been so bad. With each passing whimper from my friend, my dew-soaked t-shirt became less saturated. Every one of his phone calls shortened the length of the endless trail. My guilt toward him sold me on the idea I had not been as hungry as I told everyone I had or suffered hypothermia *and* heat exhaustion in the span of a single day. Weeks after his initial invitation and taking into consideration we wouldn't be camping out overnight, I made the conscious decision that I could handle one more afternoon in the woods. I picked up the phone. As I agreed to let him pick me up the next day, my stomach felt tight. I should have listened to my gut.

A predictable chill ran through me when the park's sign came into view. We turned and entered the forest. As I mentally prepared for my friend to stop the car so we could begin our voyage into the wild, he kept driving. Five minutes passed, then ten. We went up hills. We went down hills. He wrapped the vehicle around numerous curves. We passed campsites. He drove over more hills. All the while we descended deeper and deeper into the recesses of the forest. Just as I was starting to wonder whether my ex-girlfriend had contracted him to kill me and he had chosen to do so far enough from civilization that coyotes would consume my corpse before anyone was any the wiser, a gravel parking lot appeared out of nowhere. The car slowed to a stop, he parked, and we got out.

My friend stepped out of the vehicle, arched his back, and drew his arms over his head. Amid his full-body, cat-like stretch, he took a deep breath and audibly exhaled. "Isn't this great?" he asked, without so much as a hint of sarcasm.

I looked at him. I looked around. I muttered an acrid, "Yeah."

I then turned and was met by the trail's entrance. In the course of all of the compass-spinning twists, roller-coaster hills, and sphincter-shriveling turns, I hadn't noticed that we had stopped at the top of a very large ridge. The beginning of the trail was not pleasant, inviting, or even remotely civil; it was recreational molestation at its best. It was straight down. And the ground was composed of loose, golf ball-sized chert. The burnt orange, red, and beige-colored rocks, which were as smooth as a ball of razor wire, proceeded down the pathway as far as I could see. It was obvious. He had been hired to kill me.

After he strapped on a day bag — which I wondered what he could possibly need in such vast quantities in the forest aside from the rope, duct tape, and knife he would be using to murder me — and found a wrist-thick branch to use as a walking stick, my friend started the hike. I begrudgingly followed. As he went about his way, and without warning, he would periodically pause and whip out a folding saw from a pocket stationed on the thigh of his army

12

fatigues. He quickly cut through a gangly branch before, and with the exact same amount of advance notice, swinging the blade at some overgrown grasses that hung out over the pathway. It did not seem to bother him that my face happened to be occupying the same area as his follow-through. "Here. Smell," he demanded, as he jutted the seeping limb under my nearly severed nose. An overbearing, eye-watering odor saturated the air. "Sassafras," he declared. "They used to make root beer out of this," he added before tossing the aromatic branch off into the woods. He then neatly folded the saw, stuck it in his pocket, and proceeded happily down the trail. I squinted at the back of his head. I'd assumed my friend had taken the God-forsaken job because no one else would hire him, but now I understood that for whatever suicidal reason, he actually *liked* being in the forest.

He might as well have been whistling while skipping merrily along.

And so it went. When we came upon a steep incline, my friend would mindlessly pause, grab the top of either side of his waistline, yank up his pants, and then wriggle up the hill. I continued to follow under silent protest as I attempted to maintain my balance atop the flinty gravel beneath my feet. I foresaw myself suddenly losing my footing and falling face-first onto the serrated rocks. As I pulled my bloody face from the earth, I knew with certainty I would be devoid a few front teeth. But my friend seemed oblivious to the inherent and, in my mind, eminent dangers that surrounded us on all sides. It was clear to me that ill would inevitably befall us in the immediate future; the only unsolved variable was the degree of severity. Still, the farther along he went, the more my soon-to-be former friend reveled in being where he was.

I couldn't reconcile my reality with his attitude. Where we were was smack dab in the middle of nowhere. And from my experience, a very dangerous nowhere — the woods. I considered this the worst aspect of the very bad idea of traipsing this far into the wilderness.

Neither of us had cell phones. If something happened, we would have to wait until the next insensible person who naively walked the trail found our corpses hanging from a tree, the byproduct of a wendigo having nabbed us, strung us up, and nibbled our tasty bits before leaving the rest for the flies. Or our bodies could be discovered bloated from the mid-day heat once rigor mortis had done its work as a colony of ants slowly ebbed away at what little flesh remained on our bones *after* a bobcat lunged out of nowhere and severed all our limbs. Worse yet, we might finally be located but still alive, dragging ourselves up a chert-riddled incline because we'd stumbled across a nest of copperheads which had, out of sheer boredom, taken turns biting us until they had ran out of venom, waited for their poison glands to replenish themselves, before starting afresh until we got it through our thick heads that we didn't belong out here.

Because of the peril my friend had put me in, I started envisioning entire swarms of demon hornets appearing out of nowhere and descending upon him. I visualized him frantically dashing off into the woods, haphazardly tossing his walking stick in the air as he fled. After much zigging and zagging in the desperate attempt to evade his persecutors, he would peak a hill which happened to righteously be the end of a cliff. In my imagining, I watched as he went up and over, a wry smile on my face, as he plummeted to his annoyingly happy death.

He actually started whistling.

Eventually we came to a fork in the trail. A sign offered two choices. A green arrow pointed right. Under it someone had written "spur." A yellow arrow pointed to the left. I prayed to Artemis, the goddess of the wilderness who had graciously chosen to spare my life before, that my friend would opt to go right. He glanced back at me, said "Let's have some fun," and bumbled off to the left.

I knew this was the beginning of the end. Artemis had let me live and now I arrogantly questioned her judgment. Merely returning to the wilderness had been an insult and I subsequently bitch-slapped her by choosing to remain in the woods longer than I had to. I would undoubtedly pay for my indiscretion and intrinsically knew I would not be leaving the forest.

It did not take long to figure out Artemis' plan: She intended to kill me with boredom. It was autumn. The trees were barren and the forest floor was tiled with a mosaic of leaves. The endless expanse of monotony made it difficult to keep track of time. As I remained watchful of the dangers I knew to be all too real, I maintained a healthy distance from my friend who was off in his own little world and therefore consistently reckless with his saw blade. At some point, either I begun to lag behind or my friend's speed was proportionate to his ever-increasing spirits. If this were the case, I thought to myself, he was fueled by happiness. It wouldn't have surprised me if, any moment now, rainbows and unicorns started shooting out from his every orifice.

When I finally caught up with him, he was standing in the middle of the trail. My friend had taken off his backpack and was eagerly unwrapping a sandwich. This irritated me. I didn't think it was possible to engage in a celebratory unveiling of something wedged between two slices of bread, but he was nevertheless joyfully doing so. He had packed what all card-carrying members of the Happy Camper Club prepare for lunch: peanut butter and jelly. He offered me half, but I politely refused with a wave of my hand. He dismissively shrugged, continued to contentedly smack on his kid's meal, and gazed off in the opposite direction. This annoyed me. I saw no point in wasting the energy to bother peering off to the right or the left. It all looked the same.

He then asked if I was thirsty. Due to my expansive hiking experience, before we left I had made a point to ask him how long this particular road to perdition ran. When he told me it was only three miles, I didn't see the need to bring along a beverage because, alas, it was I who had forged 10 crippling miles without so much as breaking a sweat. However, it was only after he held up a gallon jug brimming with water that I became aware that my mouth was excessively dry. I snatched it from him and took several large gulps. I handed the jug back to him and asked why he'd brought so much to drink.

"You'll see," he said. The finality and inflection in his voice made me nervous. Had he lied to me about how long the trail was? For some inexplicable reason, I became momentarily lightheaded.

After he finished eating, he produced a small collapsible shovel from his bag. When I glanced over and noticed what he had in his hand, I inadvertently twitched and took an apprehensive step back. He unfolded it and stepped off the trail. I was alarmed. I didn't think it was permissible to leave the boundaries of the forest pathway. He moseyed back and forth along a hillside searching for something. I grew bored watching him. Because the scenery offered even less stimulation, I let my mind wander. An indeterminate time later, the sound of shuffling leaves interrupted my sporadic daydream. My friend was standing beside me wielding a smile so wide it pained me to look at him. He was holding a small cedar sapling as if it were his first trout.

"I gotta go plant this where the tornado damage broke off the trail," he proclaimed. And off he went.

Unclear as to what he meant, I followed due to a lack of anything better to do. After a brief sojourn, another fork presented itself and, without pausing, my friend amended his gait to accommodate the trail to his right. We stopped along a portion of the pathway where the trail suddenly ceased and dropped off into nothingness.

I approached the ledge, stood on my tiptoes, and leaned forward so as to safely see where it led. I was instantly nauseated. It was easily a 100-foot drop. I slowly backed away from the abyss and mentally catalogued yet another ingenious way I could die in the forest.

I walked back to where my friend was. He had dug a hole roughly five yards from the drop-off, gently planted the tree, undoubtedly fertilized it with joy, replaced the dirt, and was now slowly saturating the ground around the fledgling plant with what remained of our water. He then stood up and kicked leaves onto the trail. Pleased with his work, he stared at the sapling. He continued gawking at the plant. I decided it best to give him a moment alone with his tree and walked a few feet in the direction from which we'd come. As I waited, wondering whether he was considering asking for the cedar's bough in marriage or would just go on admiring its beauty at a polite distance, I massaged my temples and attempted to reconcile the point in moving a tree from one area to another in a place that was nothing but trees. Sensing my frustration, he turned and looked in my direction. I could feel his bubbling eyes. We'd known each other for over a decade. My problem was that he knew what I was thinking. He stood there smiling at me, goading me to say something. After a few more infuriating seconds, I gave in.

"Seriously?" I asked.

"Yeah," he blithely replied. My anger was clearly making his day all the more rewarding. We stood staring at one another. His face lit up.

"Oh," he uttered, jerking a finger up in the air indicating he wanted me to wait, "one more thing real quick." He darted past me, kicking more leaves onto the well-worn route as he went. My friend continued skipping merrily along before leaping off the trail close to where he had found the sapling. As I loathingly trudged after him, I glanced behind me. I did a double-take. It was as if the trail we'd just left had never existed: The leaves he'd shuffled onto the pathway blended seamlessly into those on the trail's periphery.

I stopped when I heard a rustling of dead foliage off in the distance. A few minutes later my friend reappeared. Without so much as a word, he smiled at me, turned, and started off down the trail. I didn't move.

"Hold on, goddammit," I demanded.

He turned around, a Cheshire grin on his face, "What?"

"You know what," I said as I nodded toward his head.

A half-dead Christmas fern had erupted from the top of his backpack.

17

"What?" he coyly asked. "This?" he said as he pointed over his shoulder.

"Yes," I replied, "*that.*"

"Almost dead. On the edge of an eroded cliff. Shriveled root system. A goner. Gonna see if I can bring her back to life," he replied before turning around and heading down the trail once more.

I sighed and started walking. I watched as the fern bobbed up and down, to and fro, with each step he took. The dried, orange plant obscured my view of his head. It looked like I was following a fraggle with a pituitary problem through the forest. Only then did it occur to me the full extent and severity of my predicament. I was stuck in the middle of the wilderness and my only hope of salvation was a happiness-fueled fraggle who farted rainbows and belched unicorns. I was a dead man.

Just as my eternal furlough from civilization was beginning to weigh on my psyche, my friend abruptly stopped ahead of me. He was parallel to the trail and looking at something toward the base of the ridge we had been traveling along. When I caught up to him, he looked at me, back down the leaf-strewn hillside, and back at me. I peered into the valley and saw nothing other than trees and leaves. I looked back at him. He raised a mischievous eyebrow and blurted out what I quickly surmised was a rhetorical question, "Wanna have some fun?" before casting himself down the incline. I didn't immediately follow because the image of the tick that had burrowed to my fibula had involuntarily sprung to mind and subsequently paralyzed me. Noticing that I had balked at his invitation, he yelled, "C'mon, this'll cut our time in half. The trail loops around." Seeing no other option because I had no clue how much of the trail remained — and since the sun was starting to set, estimated that if I turned around, I might not make it out of the forest before lions and tigers set off on their pre-dusk prowl for humans — I hesitantly stepped off the path and onto the blanket of leaves as if I was testing the temperature of a bathtub full of water, the likes of which I assumed would forever remain

18

a fond memory.

It did not take long before I deduced my friend was indeed a big, fat liar. After what I estimated to have been the passage of several hours, I gave serious consideration to feeding his fraggle fern to him if I heard the feigned reassurance of "The trail's right up here" or "Not much farther" one more time. Regardless of my terrestrial precautions as I tried to carefully plot every step I took, more often than not sheer momentum dictated my speed and direction as I chaotically danced down one hillside after another. The monumental amount of sweat I was excreting selflessly volunteered to act as a makeshift adhesive as leaves clung to my face because every other hill demanded I crawl on my hands and knees if I were to have any reasonable aspirations of flushing a toilet ever again. In spite of all of this, the trail refused to present itself. I knew we were in trouble when I somehow managed to locate my newly sworn enemy in a narrow gorge between two bourgeoning mountains.

He was squinting at a map of the park, trying to determine where we were in the early evening twilight. As he studied the map, I looked up through the barren trees and saw Venus. I no longer cared how many ticks were busily sucking away at me, draining me of my vital fluids, careening me down the shotgun barrel of anemia. As my friend mumbled parts of phrases,

". . . were *here* . . . ,"

". . . should be . . . ," and

" . . . if we were to . . . ," he would point at a hill we'd just fallen down, take an oblivious open-mouthed glance back at the map, before pivoting 90 degrees and repeating the process. I silently prayed for the beasts of the jungle to take us now. I looked around, hoping to find a suspicious gap in a hillside that screamed "nest of copperheads" so I could take a stick, shove it in the hole a handful of times, and quickly lie next to it before the pit viper exodus commenced. I would have even consented to the undignified death-by-jackalope so long as it be quick. My mind started playing tricks on me: The faint sound of dueling banjos suddenly emerged off in the distance before ominously receding into nothingness. I was ready to give up. I had it coming to me. I had arrogantly given Artemis the middle finger. I welcomed my just reward.

When my friend folded the map, stuck it in his back pocket, and started up the next miniature mountain, I seriously considered staying put. I didn't see the point. I knew we weren't ever leaving the woods. My mind flashed to my library, which had finally eclipsed being somewhat respectable. A tear welled in my eye at the thought that, upon my demise, its orphaned volumes would most likely become the innocent victims of a yard sale. When my friend yelled "C'mon," I awoke from my dream of death to find him standing at the top of another hill. For whatever subconscious reason, I trudged forward.

I do not remember leaving the forest. I don't remember the ride back into town. My first memory after surrendering to fate in a leaf-strewn, earthen crevice in the middle of the woods that I assumed was the poorly-furnished atrium to hell is of me waking up in a bathtub full of steaming hot water. I looked around. I was in my apartment. Or heaven. Or hell. It didn't matter because I wasn't in the forest any longer. Like a bad acid trip, suddenly everything came flooding back: the chert, the peanut butter and jelly sandwich, the spade, the cedar sapling . . . the fraggle fern. I had been in the woods. Deep in the woods. My mind went blank. At that exact moment my existence was incomprehensible to me. An image comprised of millions of leaves began to fill my mental vision. As my mind's eye gradually narrowed in on a single leaf, I jolted awake. Only then did I fully grasp that I had survived. Then it hit me: I had been crawling on my hands and knees through the wilderness. My deer-in-headlights glance into nothingness instantly dissipated as my eyes darted to my water-soaked legs. As I regained my focus, I jerked my knees to my nose and started inspecting my calves for ticks. Nothing. I felt all over my body. Nothing. I sank back down into the tub and a long sigh of relief escaped my lips. I had somehow not only managed to survive, but was tick free. Only then did I realize that Artemis has a soft spot for idiots.

I swore I would never return to that, or any other, forest ever again.

Chapter 3

Going Up the Country (Largely Against My Will)

I was back in the same exact forest three years later. I had done well, having held out over twice as long as I had between my first and second outings to places I sincerely believed no human being rightly belonged. My success in staying on the anti-nature wagon was due to dogged perseverance and stimulus response-induced revulsion.

I absolutely, positively, unequivocally refused to have anything to do with the outdoors. Tourette's syndrome manifested when a friend of a friend asked if I'd like to join everyone at the local conservation center. A hellfire sermon burst from my lips whenever an acquaintance suggested camping be placed on our tentative weekend itinerary. During the first few months after I'd returned from voluntarily dropping down a few links on the food chain with Fraggle Fern, I became physically ill if I caught the faintest whiff of freshly cut grass and took a detour to avoid passing the local A&W. For the first two years of my rehabilitation from the wilderness, I only permitted my feet to touch paved surfaces.

I finished graduate school and started teaching. Over time I became host to a sensible, civil, contented, nature-free existence. I had a comfy, climate-controlled apartment constructed of largely man-made materials and ate foods which were the product of science—i.e., fast food—not Mother Earth. Worshipping at the altar of the Almighty Showerhead, I paid my respects by transforming my bathroom into a water park every day before work. For the first few weeks after my return, I made a point of arbitrarily flushing the toilet merely because I could. I kept the curtains drawn in my bedroom because I had no desire to ruin the start of every day by waking up to the sight of trees. I wrote a will which specified that, should I die, not a single memorial flower was to be allowed to enter the funeral home.

I drove to campus even though my office was only four blocks away. I felt safe at work knowing I was barricaded from what I had begun to refer to as "out there." Although the cinder block walls that ensconced my classroom contained elements found *out there*, I uttered a daily sigh of relief knowing a multi-syllable synthetic composite — euphemistically referred to as "paint" — stood between us. I was probably the only faculty member to literally celebrate when the chalkboards were replaced with laminated sheets of plastic. Though the fumes of the dry erase markers were perhaps slowly eating away at the brain cells I had worked so hard to fill with knowledge, I didn't care. Their smell was the antithesis of anything remotely akin to the odor of decaying leaf matter, wet soil, or blooming flowers. I developed an aversion to darkly tanned women. As I slowly regained my confidence as a 21st-century artificial man, I made a point to sneer at our in-house environmental studies scholar at least once a day when we passed each other in the halls. I was happy because I had survived and, more importantly, I had regained control of my life. Nothing anyone could say or do and no amount of money, fame, or riches might be offered that would get me to go back into the woods ever again.

A year later, I got married to an individual who met my newly-instituted mandate that anyone I date not hike, fish, snorkel, bird watch, backpack, swim, beach comb, hunt, canoe, stargaze, pick flowers, kayak, garden, rock climb, catch butterflies, ski, surf, breathe fresh air, or willfully step outside a building unless it was on fire. Against my better judgment, Fraggle Fern had been my best man.

She was the perfect woman. She referred to camping as "crazy talk," believed group nature outings were mobile psychiatric conventions, and abhorred the smell of bonfire smoke. A veterinary technician by trade, a year into our marriage she decided to return to school and study history. A woman of impeccable taste, our mutual interests continued to align themselves once she started showing a preference for 20th-century American history. We had many discussions about the impact the Arts had on society during the time period and vice versa. Life was good. I had a wife, career, and bulging library. Not so much as a single houseplant was to be found in my home or office.

Then something bad happened.

She signed up for a topical, upper-level course focusing on the 1960s.

At the start of the term, she went on and on about L.B.J. I braced myself for the ensuing feminist movement which, when it finally arrived, didn't turn out as bad as I had expected. Perhaps it was because we were still in the early years of our marriage, she nonetheless consented to having sex with me during this tension-filled unit so long as the preconditions of doing the dishes and taking out the trash had been met. She asked me my professional opinion of the quality of Malcolm X and Martin Luther King, Jr.'s written work. By midterm, any Baby Boomer passing by our home might have had auditory-triggered flashbacks: She had purchased the remastered recording of the entire Woodstock festival. I knew Vietnam couldn't be far away. I thumbed through her biography of Nixon as a female clad in tie-dye who reminded me of my wife relayed her impressions of the Kennedy family's response to John and Robert's deaths. My clothes begun to smell of burnt pepper as a dense patchouli fog took up residence along the ceiling of our home and only subsided once the fire alarm went off. I learned that someone, somewhere mass produces patchouli-scented soap and deodorant. On nights when sleep didn't come easily, I stared up at the Buddhist prayer flags which dangled from the ceiling above our bed and counted down the days to the moon landing. I could hardly wait for Charles Manson's cult to start killing a lot of people.

I had married a hippie and didn't know it.

Then something strange happened.

I was upstairs searching through our personal papers, trying to locate our marriage certificate. I wanted to see if I'd overlooked a generational regression exemption clause. Surrounded by a battalion of stacked documents—our mortgage, insurance statements, previous years' taxes, student loans, and vehicle registrations and inspections—my concentration was broken by the sound of footsteps in the stairwell. My peace-loving roomie stopped halfway up the stairs. Although she remained out of sight, her Nosferatu shadow stretched the entire length of the wall and hung over my head. The hippie playing the part of my wife declared that we would start recycling. Without further ado, the shadow then receded to the accompaniment of fading footfalls. A slight hint of burnt pepper lingered in the air.

For the next few weeks, I entered the kitchen to find that the trashcan was trying to swallow my wife whole. Shivers ran down my spine as her arms darted maniacally in and out of the receptacle as one recyclable item after another skidded across the hardwood floor. I'd forgotten once again to set them aside and no amount of dishwashing would let me forget this. Over time, however, I adapted to a routine I didn't entirely agree with. I nonetheless reiterated to her what my initial response to the term "environmental ethics" had been when I was in college: "It's dirt. Who cares?" My position hadn't wavered.

Not long after, a small, blue container appeared on the kitchen counter. I was told it was our compost bucket, the counterpart of which I would begin building immediately if not sooner. Two days later I escorted our inaugural collection of onion peels, carrot tops, and coffee grounds to our newest mowing hazard: a haphazardly, poorly-constructed compost bin held together by ten-penny nails, duct tape, and hope.

It was about this time I noticed our grocery bill had suddenly started going up, but saw no proportional influx in volume. When I inquired as to what she was buying in bulk or had been prey to late frosts earlier that year, my wife stared at me, not comprehending what I was asking. I mentioned I'd glanced at the last few grocery receipts. She uttered a noncommittal "Oh," before sauntering into the living room. Then the phrase "organic is more expensive" echoed down the hallway.

I had married an environmentalist and didn't know it.

I knew without having to look that there was no tree hugging indemnity clause, even in the fine print of our marriage certificate. But we'd been manacled together in the Catholic Church. I wondered if I could get some leverage with the religious institution if I pinned my wife with the label of nature-worshipping Wiccan or possibly even Druid.

In the end, I surrendered. I was simply stuck with my little dirt apostle. Perhaps a foreseeable inevitability, John Denver and Marvin Gaye gradually replaced Jimi Hendrix and Janis Joplin. I was somewhat glad that The Beatles managed to make the transition, but with my background in the Arts, it should have occurred to me something was thematically afoot. Perhaps I did and my subconscious wilderness filter kept me from seeing it. Admittedly, when the nasally "Going Up the Country" by Canned Heat made its way into my wife's daily music rotation, a sensible person would have taken out an ad in the local paper inquiring if anyone was readily available and interested in an affair with a strapping, comparably young literature professor with a tick scar and soon-to-be ex-wife.

But I persisted as the dutiful, faithful, supportive husband despite Dr. Seuss' *The Lorax* having become one of my involuntarily choices for bathroom reading. When I complained about the music or the dense patchouli miasma, both of which made my eyes water, my wife simply quoted, "For better or worse." It was only then that I realized the phrase was not multiple-choice.

Approximately two-and-a-half years after I had taken her hand in marriage, my wife peeped her head around the door that lead to my study. It was a droll, leisurely Sunday afternoon and I was contentedly grading the first round of papers from an 8-week online summer class I had just started teaching. Without bothering to wait for me to look up, she said — less as a question than a thought to be batted around — "Why don't we go hiking?"

I stopped what I was doing, reached for a pen and paper, and begun drafting my singles ad before browsing the Internet for local divorce lawyers. I might have been able to pinpoint the catalyst for my wife's seemingly innocent, bachelor-producing request if I would have chosen to continue studying philosophy instead of literature. A dog-eared copy of Rachel Carson's 1962 environmental fire alarm *Silent Spring* had migrated around the house since the close of the previous term. I decided it best not to pointlessly risk playing the role of the nay-saying husband if there was a chance the question might dissipate on its own accord. I prayed her newfound passion was a passing phase, especially in light of her previous dislike for the outdoors.

I soon discovered that the Greek myth of Pandora's Box was wrong. Hope *had* escaped. The weeks passed, but the cursory statement did not. Instead, it slowly metamorphosed into a direct, pointed question that flitted around my head every other day. I knew I had to bottleneck, if not outright suffocate, my wife's stillborn request. I sat her down at the kitchen table. This was a nonverbal signal both of us recognized as precipitating a serious discussion. I hoped that my choice of conversational venues would speak for itself.

Again, Pandora's Box.

Even though I was trained in and taught the art of rhetoric, my approach was stereotypically Western and very, very male. I entered discussions in a straightforward, pragmatic, and linear fashion. My wife's dialectic path was more subtle and had a comparatively Eastern bent. It was fraught with jagged, abrupt twists and sudden, unnavigable turns and was expressly designed to allow her rival to defeat himself. She masterfully utilized nonverbal cues to subconsciously influence her conversational adversary and instead of opening with her strongest line of reasoning, she elected to chink away at her opposition, not unlike a boxer judiciously wearing down a much larger opponent over

15 rounds before delivering the deathblow. Her strategy was nothing short of inspired.

I started out gently, simultaneously feeling her out while hoping she'd establish flimsy argumentative groundwork which could be quickly and easily dismantled.

"I wanna talk to you about this whole hiking thing. Why do you want to go hiking all of a sudden?"

"Well," she began, drawing out the word so as to drench it in sympathy-inducing emotion, "I just thought it'd be nice for us to get out of the house and do something different for a change."

Clever.

She had chosen to start by rolling the baseball over home plate. My wife was balking, hoping I'd inadvertently show my hand. Both she and I knew this was her go-to opener for any new activity she wanted us to try together. As such, I was expected to lethargically lob a response at her as we gradually worked up an oratory sweat.

To the argumentatively uninitiated, a much more intricate psychological parleying had already begun. Politicians, attorneys, lobbyists, and anyone who has been married for more than a day knows that contained within its first sentences are the seeds of a discussion's finale. Our opening statements indicated the strength and intention of both sides. Only two lines into the conversation, I had made it clear I was going to stand firm and was prepared to use every item in my rhetorical toolbox to keep from going hiking. Conversely, she was playing coy, which was indicative that she meant to dodge my Rogerian jabs and *reductio ad absurdum* left hooks for however many rounds it took until I collapsed from exhaustion.

I was leery. Her debut statement only had a median success rate. My debate senses started to tingle. Something didn't feel right. Was this a ploy? I wasn't sure. I attempted to scrutinize her facial expression, hoping the slightest twinge would give me an indication of the path she planned on taking. She held her gaze like a card shark. I thoughtfully stroked my bottom lip to buy me time but, alas, my mind was blank. As I tried to regain my focus, the image of the single, solitary leaf that had filled my mental vision when I was recuperating in my bathroom years ago flashed before my eyes.

I had to do — to say — something. I had been out of the batter's box far too long. If I didn't jump back in soon, my prolonged hesitation would trumpet my confusion. If this occurred, I would be black flagged. A single bead of sweat started forming along my hairline. I dared not wipe it away. Doing so would draw her attention to it and betray my empty hand. She had yet to notice because her left eyebrow hadn't suspiciously risen, thereby indicating my defeat. Epochs passed between ticks of the kitchen clock.

"Fine, we'll go."

I had willfully folded. Between flashes of decaying foliage as I desperately searched for a direction to take, but fearful each one had already been barricaded, I had pieced together the rationalization that I was burning energy I would need for the trail we would inevitably be traveling down in the immediate future. Although consent meant my imminent demise, I reasoned that, all things considered, I'd lived a good life and that I might as well go out on a high note.

"Yea!" she yelled, bolting upright. My wife started hopping up and down and clapping. It was her signature victory applause where she held the base of her palms together and only her fingertips touched. The barely discernable noise her hands made was mockingly disproportionate to the scale of her triumph. This was enacted with express purpose, as was her instant transformation into a giddy 14-year-old girl. She adopted this persona to ensure the total and absolute eradication of any vestiges of dignity I might have retained after being rhetorically bested. She skipped up and out of the kitchen and disappeared somewhere into the confines of the house.

Like a chess grandmaster that has been mated in less than 10 moves, I remained at the kitchen table, stunned and unable to move. As I attempted to reconcile my defeat alongside my impending death, I pushed my chair back, propped my elbows on my knees, and plunged my head into my sweaty hands. I started to calculate the potential marital repercussions of running over her compost bin with the lawnmower.

Canned Heat began playing in the background.

When we hit the city limits, I gazed longingly into the rearview mirror and bid farewell to civilization. As my wife and I went up to the country, my mind floated back to my previous, anguished time in the wilderness. It was then I recalled how large my ex-girlfriend's circle of associates had been. Was it possible my marriage was all a front? After I managed to survive my outing with the human fraggle, my ex-girlfriend undoubtedly surmised that my survival instinct was greater than she'd originally thought. Might she have devised a long-term hit which included the ruse of matrimony to get me to drop my guard?

I looked over at my wife. She sat contentedly in the passenger seat with a smile on loan from my former best friend. Regardless of whether she was my ex-girlfriend's clandestine accomplice, her grin's coincidental timing and similarity bore ominous overtones. So as not to betray that I'd unveiled the plot, I used my peripheral vision to make sure her hand didn't begin to slowly ease its way into her purse in pursuit of a razor-sharp knife. I covertly watched as she ironically bobbed her head back and forth to Joni Mitchell's lyrical announcement that Eden had been bulldozed and now played host to a parking lot.

If the person I was sitting next to was a world-renowned hired gun, she was good. Very, very good. She was diligently maintaining her cover by assuming the role of my innocent wife until my last agonizing moments. I tried to look on the bright side. Professional mercenaries always make sure their hits are quick and clean. I took solace knowing the untraceable, fatal poison used to kill me would leave my corpse in a respectable condition and my body would therefore be presentable to the general public. I hoped a lot of people would come to the funeral. I prayed no one would bring flowers.

"Look!" my wife shouted.

I temporarily lost control of the car. As I envisioned my friends peering lovingly down at me resting peacefully in my synthetic coffin, each wiping a tear from their eye as they said goodbye to me one last time before getting into a debate about who was the rightful heir to my signed, first edition paperback copy of William Burroughs' *Junkie*, I'd forgotten the person who would be my undoing happened to be sitting a mere two feet from me.

She was leaning forward in her seat and pointing out the window. Her finger remained fixed on something on the approaching hillside as I attempted to reposition the vehicle back between the painted solid line to my right and the white hyphens on the left. "A cow," she added, turning in her seat as we rolled past a contented bovine which, at that point, stood a much better chance of seeing tomorrow than I did. After the mobile hamburger faded in the distance, my wife swiveled around to face front once more.

"I like cows," she proclaimed, more to herself than me.

I glanced over at her. Again, the contented smile. Not wry. Not mocking. Contented. She had not meant this to be funny. She was either making a declarative statement affirming her bohemian fondness for all living creatures great and small or was still very much in character. Regardless, I was a dead man. A *very* dead man.

The proper course of action for anyone in my position would have been to reach across the vehicle — all the while ignoring my passenger's repeated inquiries of what I was in fact doing — open the door, and push my flower child assassin onto the speeding pavement. But I didn't because we were nearing the park. It was clear she intended to kill me deep within the woods. It made sense. Ending my life now would have been an inconvenience since I was the one driving.

I ceased to worry once the forest's tree line came into view. I had a feather in my cap which she didn't know about. Long before I'd figured out my wife's true identity, due to my expansive wilderness experience, I had taken precautions. Unfortunately my experience wasn't vast enough.

Woody Allen once said, "If you want to make God laugh, tell him about your plans." I had come to accept the very real possibility that if a benevolent God did exist, he took his lunch breaks whenever I entered the woods. My mistake was not wondering who filled in for him.

The Monday following the weekend I signed my death certificate by agreeing to take my wife hiking, I called the closest state park which, as Fate fiendishly decreed, was the same one Fraggle Fern had drug me to years before. An overly-bubbly individual answered the phone. I asked which trail was the shortest and its location. After being graciously thanked for my interest in the glorious wonders the natural world provided, I was told the briefest foray was a mere half-mile jaunt designed for senior citizens and children. It was the first trail upon entering the park. Fifteen minutes later—after I had been involuntarily informed of which flowers were currently in bloom, the various types of trees that lined the microtrail, and, thank God, that the footpath was almost consistently level throughout—the voice on the other end of the line began to outline the park's prolonged history. Somewhere around the 30-minute mark, my mental image of a person wearing forest green canvas Daisy Dukes, gray wool socks and hiking boots, and a beige button-up with perhaps suspenders that complemented his shorts shifted to a picture of me standing over the granola muncher, my hands wrapped firmly around his neck as his ponytail, which smelled vaguely of pinecones and environmental enthusiasm, swung back and forth with each life-depriving jerk of my arms.

I would live to teach another day because the trail we would be hiking was too short and risked others hearing my tormented cries if my wife tried to off me.

But my pre-hike preparations were all in vain.

If I had been paying attention, once the all-too-familiar yellow lettering on the square, brown sign broadcasting the park's entrance came into view and flippantly welcomed one and all, I would have discovered who covered for God when he went to the bathroom. Pandora threw back her head and committed to a guttural laugh as we drove past the visitor center, behind which resided the half-mile trail. Tears undoubtedly streamed down her face as I kept driving, waiting for a gravel parking lot to spring up on either my right or left, thereby announcing the first of the park's designated pathways. By the time my wife and I stepped out of the car and into the humid July heat as we unwittingly faced a three-mile descent into the underworld which had a "challenge" rating of 9 out of 10, I suspect Pandora was doubled-over in pain from laughing too hard. She might have even lost bladder control when my wife asked if I'd brought along any water and I victoriously informed her that there was no need because I'd called ahead; we'd be off the trail which lay before us in less than half an hour.

I suppose it was possible that the park employee had made a point to mention the trail I so desperately sought hadn't been given its own visual marker due to its brevity. If he had indeed specified the senior citizen walkway was on the left and not the right of the park's entrance, thereby saving my life in the process, the utterance had been lost amid his disclosure of the mating habits of tree frogs and the average wind speed of the park in 1891. But I suspect he hadn't. In retrospect I believe he had deliberately omitted these facts because he was working alongside my wife's employer as Operation Kill Mike drew to a close. Either that or he worshipped at the shrine of Pandora, who had sent him to do her bidding. If this were indeed the case, she had demanded nothing less than a human sacrifice.

Because it was many, many hours before sunset, I followed the lead of my best friend and took the time to carefully select a downed branch to serve as my walking stick while my wife doused herself in what wouldn't have surprised me was patchouli-scented bug spray. I intended to keep the bough as a souvenir if the day unfolded as I expected, its culmination being me tossing an extended middle finger to the forest as I set off back into town, taking both my life and previously purloined dignity with me.

Just as my wife proclaimed she was ready to begin, I brushed aside the observation that the trail's threshold harbored trees which hung ominously over the pathway's entrance in ready anticipation of closing off a gullible hiker's only escape route. I refused to place any particular importance upon how the trail seemed to grow darker the farther we meandered into its depths despite it being mid-day. No mental red flags were raised when we came to our first incline, which ran approximately 45 degrees, because—I reconciled—a trail's severity is relative. Perhaps the park employee I'd spoken to was a veteran hiker. The reason I didn't take these matters seriously was that my mindset was contaminated by the assurances I had taken to make this outing as brief and pain-free as possible. I now know that if I were indeed the intelligent person I believed myself to be, I would have turned around, got back in my car, and left the woods straight away. But I am not, after all, a smart person.

After refusing to acknowledge something was amiss once we'd ascended three progressively steep inclines, I abandoned any suspicions that my wife was part of a coup whose sole purpose was to see me dead. We'd just finished tiptoeing along a brief but very narrow ridge. With the slightest push, my body would have lain broken and battered in the rock-lined base 50 feet below. I knew that underneath the eye-raping tie-dye and behind the dense cloud of patchouli funk, my bride had rejoined me at the anti-nature altar at the exact same moment my sustained illusion that we were on the right trail disintegrated: Mother Nature's intern complained that her thighs were burning. A notorious assassin would not expose a weakness shortly before snuffing out a target. Though I was safe from a *Mr. and Mrs. Smith*-esque demise, her grievance made it undeniable that I literally wasn't out of the woods quite yet because unless the retirees of the region were former Olympians, something was desperately wrong. I was forced to contend with reality as it now stood. Like Orpheus, I had willfully entered Hades and, like its property owner, hell took many shapes and forms. As before, instead of fire and brimstone, I was once more engulfed by rocks, trees, and hills which were cast amid a backdrop of green. As I looked around and tried to assess my situation, my wife screamed.

"Ick!" (She actually yelled "Ick!") "Get it off, get it off!" my wife frantically demanded as she spasmodically leapt backward time and again in hopes of freeing herself from the clutches of an unseen enemy. I ran over to her. "Get it off goddammit!" she screamed as she pointed between her breasts. A tick clung to the epicenter of the spiral color wheel of her shirt. Equally terrified, I snatched up a twig and—due to the heightened circumstances—failed to take guilty pleasure in where I'd quickly positioned my hands. Like a doctor performing delicate brain surgery, my tongue crept out from between my lips as I carefully wedged the stick under the parasite and flicked it away. My wife made sure to track the bug's trajectory and ran over to where it had landed. She jumped up and down several times before plunging her toe in the dank, moist soil and, with great force, swung her heel back and forth to ensure her persecutor's demise.

Exasperated, my wife looked up at me and pleaded, "How much further? Seems like we've already gone half a mile or whatever you'd said." Less due to fear of admitting I had taken us on the wrong trail and more firmly rooted in the fact I didn't want to contemplate that the remainder of our marriage might involve her gathering wild edibles as I hunted wooly mammoths, I simply told her that I did not know. I glanced down the path from which we'd come and then up the trail that lay before us. Although this action merely resulted in me getting two eyefuls of indistinguishable green things, I hoped this would mentally reassure her that I had things under control. Without knowing the length of the trail, there was no way of determining the shorter route. I proceeded along the narrow path without saying a word after coming to the conclusion that by going forward instead of backward, we at least stood the chance of seeing something new and interesting before we died.

As the day progressed, the oppressive summer heat was cheered on by the vapid humidity that clung to us like leeches, which I suspected would be making their entrance at any moment. I had long since cast my walking stick into a ravine. As it made its silent descent, I felt slightly envious of its fate. We nonetheless sallied forth although our pace and conversation dissipated with each step. As minutes melted into what seemed like days where the sun never set, we plodded on, checking off one ecosystem and landscape after another. The environment was more hostile than any I'd ever encountered. Insidious jungles gave way to alligator-infested swamps which became prairies full of lions' dens that transformed into blistering rattlesnake deserts before growing into sheer mountain ranges. Each step served as a painful reminder that I had made the wrong decision. If I would have chosen to retrace our steps instead of charting unknown territory, we would have already been home and the question of whether my family name would be carried on wouldn't have been a serious contingency to consider. Because of this, I dared not glance back at my wife. I merely assumed that, should she and I survive, once we were released from the hospital after being treated for heatstroke, divorce papers would be presented alongside my medical bill. And at that particular moment in my life I was content with the possibility because I couldn't really blame her. My only remaining concern was whether she'd get my library in the alimony settlement.

Then something strange happened. If it had been the work of a mere mortal, because it was the third such occasion wherein a miracle had taken place, the person responsible would automatically qualify for sainthood. We arrived at a junction. I stopped and looked around to make sure my dehydration-induced migraine wasn't playing tricks on my mind. The fork looked familiar but, try as I might, I couldn't recall having ever chosen to go right or left at any particular point during our voyage. A moment later, I knew we had crossed this path because a few feet away was the divot my wife had made with her toe as she put an eight-legged vampire into an early grave. My future ex-wife then stumbled into the back of me. She had dispensed with wasting the energy to look around and instead was preoccupied with making sure her tired feet didn't trip over exposed roots, which were set at precise 10-foot intervals, whose sole purpose was to antagonize and harass the asinine individuals most people refer to as hikers.

"Look honey," I said with a surprising amount of energy, energy brought about by the newfound wellspring of hope because I had long since burned every fat cell in my body. "We've already been here. This means the car's right around the corner," I told her as I pointed down the trail.

"Great," she said, her voice equal parts monotone apathy toward life and barely contained husband-directed disdain, "let's go." She brushed past me and headed toward the exit without another word.

With salvation in sight, I took off after her. Perhaps it was due to a lack of water, rampant fatigue, or knowing I probably wouldn't be seeing much of her after the separation, I decided to subtly remind her that it had been her idea to go into the woods. Like a spent marathon runner who speeds up during the final mile, I buzzed around her pointing out things we'd missed when we'd entered the trail.

"Look at this cool spider web," I said as I crouched down in the middle of the trail, deliberately blocking her path.

"Fuck your spider," she mumbled as she stepped around me without breaking her gait.

A few hundred yards later, the sentinel trees which had menacingly threatened to close in behind us receded ever so slightly and framed irrefutable evidence of a just God: our beautiful, beautiful car. Too exhausted to offer an epitaph to our joint, near-death experience, we opened the doors and fell into the vehicle. I started the car and turned the air conditioner on full blast. Like a trauma victim who had just witnessed the slaughter of millions, my wife merely sat there and stared mindlessly ahead. After backing the car out of the parking lot and putting it in drive, I rolled down the window. I flung out my arm and extended my middle finger as we drove away.

Weeks later, once it became clear that for whatever reason my wife had decided not to divorce me, I inquired about her impressions of the forest. She simply swore she would never return. I nodded in complete, total, and utter agreement.

Chapter 4

Blame Hank

We were back in the same forest four years later. The two of us probably would have abided by our renunciation of the wilderness if one, just one, of my philosophy professors would have cracked a smile. They were the reason I had arrived at and was teaching literature and the metaphorical blood will remain on their hands. Unfortunately for me, the literal blood was my own.

I had entered college with the intention of becoming a professional philosopher. Although I was perpetually rewarded by a barrage of ideas provided by guys with funny names that everyone outside of the field phonetically molested — Heraclitus, Socrates, Descartes, Leibniz, Kant, Nietzsche, Derrida — I discovered philosophy had not one, but *two* Achilles' heels. The first is that, on average, philosophers are quite simply horrible writers. Most get to the point fairly quickly, but a large majority are fearful their ideas aren't getting across, so many of the great philosophic works are painstakingly redundant.

The other problem was, from my shallow experience, there appeared to be an unspoken prerequisite to becoming a professional philosopher that had nothing to do with coursework or theoretical understanding. It seemed as if, in order to get paid to sit around and think all day, I would need to have my personality surgically removed. More precisely, philosophers simply refuse to see the humor in things. This drove me crazy, but I knew this lack of character was the byproduct of hubris. The people I read, those who taught me, and my fellow philosophy majors all labored under the notion (more than the mere mental peons whose existences they were graciously attempting to improve through their superior intellectual acumen) that they had a monopoly on being right. They were the dictators of thought. It didn't help that in all the pictures of the famed philosophers, not a single one bears so much as a wry smirk with the exception of one, Michel Foucault. It was only after I did a little research into the French thinker's personal life that I came to understand why.

I knew that if I wasn't permitted to laugh at the Laputan importance philosophers placed upon whether a color had to be attached to an object in order to be perceived, I would go insane. So I added a major. Literature was my answer. It afforded me a venue wherein I could have my ideas and giggle at them too. Novelists, short story writers, and poets knew how to laugh, but also frequently made themselves the butt of their own jokes — something no proud, self-respecting philosopher would ever be caught doing. These cut-ups, jesters, and merry pranksters of the written page simply refused to take life, or even themselves, too seriously. Though these authors often went to great, sometimes frustrating lengths to candy-coat their ideas in clever little narratives, they were nevertheless there; all a person had to do was dig a little. The icing on the cake was, unlike with philosophic tomes, I would be entertained by a story while I thought about things.

The history of literature is chock-full of comedians, satirists, parodists, farce writers, and black humorists. For me, however, a treasure trove of laughs seemed to be concentrated in one area, American literature. Admittedly Cervantes, Chaucer, Shakespeare, Voltaire, Swift, Sterne, Carroll, Wilde, Shaw, Joyce, and Beckett all have their moments but star-spangled Samuel Clemens, better known as Mark Twain, started a tradition hinted at by Melville that is still going strong today. In spite of this, there is a sad hiccup in the annals of written American comedy. There are fleeting moments in Howells, Poe, and James, but the Lost Generation led by Hemingway and Fitzgerald doesn't have a funny bone between the lot of them. Fortunately the good times start rolling again with Joseph Heller's *Catch-22* and don't stop. Postmodern American writers have an admiration bordering on the compulsive when it comes to the ha-ha: Kurt Vonnegut, William Gaddis, Thomas Pynchon, John Barth, Donald Barthelme, David Foster Wallace, Michael Chabon, Chuck Palahniuk, and Jonathan Lethem all promised me a chuckle with the turn of every page.

I have since become a little easier on philosophers in general, but on rare occasions I'm reminded of why I walked away. Just as I was beginning to collect my notes for this book, a friend introduced me to a former classmate of his. The individual was finishing his bachelor's in philosophy. Less than five minutes into the conversation, he vocalized what I assumed many of my former philosophy peers had been thinking, "I get the impression that if I sat down with you for a couple of hours, I could change the entire way you see the world." Perhaps he could, yet I had serious doubts as to his ability to shift my perspective about people who call themselves philosophers.

Although I had my graduate degree, like a dutiful scholar, I continued to study. Having most of the major American writers of the 19th and 20th centuries under my belt, I started to go back and read the secondary and minor names in the field. As I did so, I begrudgingly consented to cracking open the few major works I had perpetually put off for one reason or another. One of the books which had slipped through my bibliographical cracks was Henry David Thoreau's *Walden*.

I had postponed reading the classic for one simple reason. I had been told not to, *twice*. When I inquired about the transcendental benchmark early in my college career, one Ivy League philosophy professor assured me a basic understanding of self-sufficiency, which is one of the book's central ideas, was adequate. This was seconded by the chair of the English department, who told me, "Don't bother." Having heeded my professors' advice for over a decade, I was now beginning to feel guilty. Every time I entered the campus library, I diverted my gaze from the façade where Thoreau's name jeered at me as I passed under Homer, Milton, and Goethe with impunity.

It didn't occur to me until years later that my mentors' biases might have been because they too were hylophobic. *Walden* is often labeled the first great work of nature writing. My professors' trepidation toward the outdoors needn't have been as severe as my own, wherein if someone mumbled "ladybug" in general conversation, a panic attack set in, but it nonetheless made sense. Professional bookworms retire to their *studies*. We aren't exactly the poster children for wilderness adventures. Not one of my colleagues ever stated she was looking forward to the end of the semester because it would finally avail her to being able to go over the hills and through the woods before sitting down with a good book. A very large percentage of literature scholars are rather fond of their overstuffed recliners, artificial lighting, and easily accessible refrigerators full of animals that no longer move on their own accord. I completely understood and empathized.

So I had finally deemed it time to scratch ol' Henry David off my reading list. Over summer break I prepared a glass of sweet tea, made sure there was an ample supply of dead things in my freezer, flopped lengthways across my obese couch, switched on a nearby lamp, and picked up the two-dollar paperback of *Walden* I'd purchased years before. I took a deep, reluctant breath, held it for a second, exhaled, and opened to the first page.

"When I wrote the following pages . . . ."

I stopped immediately.

Good God, I thought as I folded the cover back over my index finger which was holding the book open. I hated first-person narratives. I quickly thumbed to the back of the text to see how long I would be expected to persevere through another self-absorbed memoir. I moaned. The book was over 200 pages.

I took another deep breath and reasoned that if I had managed to make it through Thomas Mann's *The Magic Mountain* — a rambling, 700-page sedative about a whiney, narcissistic goldbricker who, if he would have either gotten off his lazy butt and found a job or, better yet, simply died, he would have saved countless numbers of literature students a lot of unnecessary pain and suffering — I could make it through this. I opened the book once more.

By the end of the first paragraph, I got along a little better with Thoreau. After admitting he'd naively chosen to live alone in the woods for two years, common sense got the better of him because he'd since returned to "civilized life again." Okay, so — like me — Hank had made a mistake and learned from it.

I kept reading.

By the end of the first chapter, my life had been changed. *Walden* is not about how terrible the wilderness is but how it provides mental refuge for an animal that has only recently traded its natural home for aluminum siding, "For the improvements of ages have had but little influence on the essential laws of man's existence; as our skeletons, probably, are not to be distinguished from those of our ancestors." The chapter's title, "Economy," refers to both the financial as well as spiritual. Humans spend too much capital on frivolities in both areas. But Thoreau makes it abundantly clear that only after we divest ourselves of the arbitrary noise and distraction of modern living can we return to the sanctity of our natural homes both physically and, more important, mentally: "Not till we are lost, in other words not till we have lost the world, do we begin to find ourselves, and realize where we are and the infinite extent of our relations." Thoreau's words hadn't lost their meaning or influence 150 years later. I had heard this line paraphrased in a movie my students constantly talked about, David Fincher's *Fight Club*: "It's only after we've lost everything that we're free to do anything."

If what Thoreau said was true, I was far from finding myself. I was irrefutably a model for postmodern consumerism. I had a terminal case of affluenza. I owned entire shelves of books, music, and movies whose titles were hidden under a wooly layer of dust. Boxes of indistinguishable, nondescript "stuff" sat dormant in both my basement and attic. Cute little trinkets could be found in every corner of every room. Self-identification was impossible because I was buried under a pile of unnecessary, arbitrary, useless things. I intrinsically understood Thoreau's parable of the doormat, "A lady once offered me a mat, but as I had no room to spare within the house, nor time to spare within or without to shake it, I declined it, preferring to wipe my feet on the sod before my door. It is best to avoid the beginnings of evil." I realized the saddest part was not how much time I'd invested in earning money to buy these superfluous items, whose total cost made me lightheaded as I tallied their estimated sum in my head, but that I didn't cherish their vicarious value, my spent life, enough to bother maintaining them. If owning frivolous articles of excess were indeed the trappings of malevolence, my home was ready to play host to the Axis powers.

At least Ozymandias had a statue erected in his name. If I were to have died at that moment, the only thing I had managed to erect in my honor was a shrine to China's manufacturing capabilities.

I was amazed by Thoreau's thinking, but also admired his prose. I had never read anyone so naturally inclined toward extended metaphor, known in literature as the art of conceit. Although non-fiction, his writing is poetic, nay, beautiful in its presentation and the eloquence of its poignant brevity left me speechless. Instead of continuing on to the next chapter, I flipped back to the beginning of the book. It looked like I'd dipped the American classic in a vat of red ink: Without realizing it, I'd underlined almost every other sentence. I nevertheless reread the gospel according to H.D.T.

I finished *Walden* in the wee hours of the following morning. My eyes came to the last line, "The sun is but a morning star," and I eagerly turned the page to begin another glorious chapter. My heart sank when I was met by a blank page. Only then did it occur to me that I'd been so consumed by what I was reading, I hadn't noticed how thin the right side of the book had become.

Sadly, despite my perspective upon the outdoors and our place within it having changed, I gave myself an alibi for not putting theory into practice. I told myself that I was simply too busy. I was teaching in three departments for two colleges. However, although the initial impact of *Walden* was gradually diluted by other authors' words and the encumbrances of daily life,

Thoreau's ghost leaned over my shoulder whenever I got ready to make another house payment. I could hear the transcendentalist sucking knowing air through his teeth, "tsk, tsk, tsk," before hanging his head in disappointed shame. One of his chosen apostles had defected. Instead of standing up to live, I sat down to write another check. As I scribbled my name in the bottom, right corner of the rectangular piece of paper, he whispered in my ear, "And when the farmer has got his house, he may not be the richer but the poorer for it, and it be the house that has got him." *Fight Club*'s main character said much the same, "The things you own, end up owning you." I looked down. Before me sat a document which I had just signed that confirmed I was shackled to a house, car, and therefore my job. I was definitely owned.

I nevertheless continued jumping through flaming bureaucratic hoops and limboing under political red tape at work. But instead of doing so with passive reluctance, I started to actively wonder what I was doing it for. I was wasting the better portion of my life earning money that I hoped to enjoy during the least valuable part of it. This irony plagued my philosophical mind. The image of a new convertible veering wildly into a parking spot before a humpbacked, gray-headed retiree pushes open the door and gingerly places his walker onto the pavement forced its way into my nightly dreams. But I was nowhere near what society deemed the apex of life, the golden years of retirement. As such, I asked myself what my life would amount to if I were T-boned by a student on the way to class. It became clear to me that the deathbed regret is what unveils the value of life: A billionaire's dying words are never "I wish I'd spent more time at the office." People lament about lost time with family, adventures not taken, and personal goals that weren't achieved. They always grieve about not having lived a life worth talking about. In its place is a squandered existence wherein one day — of a person's own as well as everyone else's — was indistinguishable from the next.

I wasn't even midway through my autobiography. The thought that at any moment the *Book of Me* might be prematurely abandoned before I'd had the opportunity to begin penning the appendix sent chills down my spine. Even scarier was the fact that the book wouldn't be that interesting.

Although the months, and then years, marched on, Thoreau stayed with me unlike any other author. The reason was obvious. Aside from finally being able to taste the forbidden fruit of his writing after so many years, unlike other philosophers, H.D.T. had provided me with practical advice which could improve my quality of life. Whether the color red could stand alone had no bearing on if I was happy with who I was; whether my moment-to-moment existence was consumed by "factitious cares and superfluously coarse labors" did. Thoreau had hit the nail on the head. I had been misled, not by philosophers (who, he correctly observes, had ceased to exist eons ago), but rather professors of philosophy. I now saw the distinction.

Like a discontent parent trying to live vicariously through one's children, I pushed my suppressed aspirations onto my students. I did this while telling myself that since they had chosen the same path, I was merely attempting to keep the next generation from winding up like me, a white-collar marionette. I assigned wilderness hikes and, for once, eagerly evaluated the stories of their lives. We frequently read segments from Thoreau aloud in class:

> *Which would have advanced the most at the end of the month, – the boy who had made his own jackknife from the ore which he had dug and smelted, reading as much as would be necessary for this – or the boy who had attended the lectures on metallurgy at the Institute in the meanwhile, and had received a Rodgers penknife from his father? Which would be more likely to cut his fingers?*

I listened to myself and my colleagues extol the values and concepts found in literature. Though we had a theoretical understanding of what we spoke about, it became clear to me I hadn't a clue as to what they meant or how they related to my life. My respected position offered me the mind-numbing safety of routine and shielded me from genuine, potentially life-changing events. Although I navigated down the same river of life as Huck Finn, my bank account ensured the tides would remain docile. My Hamletian hesitations were limited to when I couldn't decide how to vote during faculty meetings. Ahab's obsession dwarfed my comparatively inconsequential concern of which tie to wear in case the dean spotted me at a faculty luncheon. Because returning home to my wife merely involved getting in my car and turning the key, Odysseus' epic voyage back to his beloved Penelope was doomed to remain a flaccid story on the page. Regardless of how many times I read Tolstoy, I couldn't appreciate the true value of peace because I had never experienced war outside a student contesting a grade. The only benefit of my newfound existential dilemma was that I now understood Faust's plight: I'd contractually agreed to surrender much more than my time and labor by signing my teaching contract.

I also realized why Hollywood's stock character for boredom was the English professor. I had chosen a life based around literature, tales of other people's adventures, because I didn't have a page-worthy life of my own. Instead of sucking the marrow out of life, I had satisfied myself with nibbling the leftovers of those who had the courage to go out and live. Although a portion of American authors had lived the writer's life of telling other people's tales, many transcribed their own adventures, both literally and metaphorically. Jack London faced the Great White North, Conrad and Melville were seamen, Vonnegut and Heller had seen war, Kerouac and Ginsberg traveled the U.S. I was, at best, an armchair adventurer too afraid to step outside. I didn't even *know* any interesting, narrative-quality people. All of my acquaintances were carbon copies of me whose lives differed by inconsequential matters of detail. I was living a vicarious life of quiet, hypocritical desperation.

My autobiography would be about as interesting as a bowl of soggy bran flakes.

On the first page of *Walden*, Thoreau states, "I trust that none will stretch the seams in putting on this coat [the book itself], for it may do good service to him whom it fits." I was surprised at how well Thoreau conformed to my thinking from the beginning, albeit his philosophy was a bit snug under the arms. However, as I grew more and more discontented with my redundant, consumer lifestyle, the transcendental jacket grew to fit my form.

During a bored weekday amid yet another Christmas Break, I settled in at the kitchen table with my tattered copy of *Walden*. Since that fateful long evening when I first encountered Hank, I had read his entire canon, personal letters, biographies, and the greater part of available scholarship on the writer. Yet *Walden* remained my perennial favorite. As I thumbed back and forth between my pet sections, portions of which I could now quote at length, I suddenly stopped. I stared blankly in the distance. I was on the verge of a life-changing epiphany. My Thoreauvian coat was about to look tailor-made.

As I sat there, pondering the moral consequences of what I read, a well-known thought experiment came to mind. The societal value of one's vocation can be distilled by placing it alongside others on a desert island. Aside from being a storyteller, I quickly deduced that once I had run out of yarns to keep my co-islanders entertained after a hard day's labors, I would serve one purpose and one purpose only, food. It was at that moment I decided I no longer wanted to be the person who talked about other people for a living, fictional or otherwise. I definitely didn't want to be the person whom others remembered as having been "a bit lean, maybe a tad overdone" as they picked remnants of me out from between their teeth.

I understood that the rest of my life might well be comparable to Francis Macomber's—a Hemingway character who finds happiness mere seconds before his premature death—but at least I wouldn't wind up the poor, pitiful, arthritic old man trying to vainly capture his lost youth through an overpriced sports car which he drove to prostate exams who, on his deathbed, wished he'd done something else with his life.

After my resolution, the first thing I did was sit down with a pen and paper. I set to adding up my monthly expenditures because I had no real idea how much the essentials of mortgage, insurance, a car payment, utilities, and groceries ran every 30 days. I gathered all my bills together, tallied the sum, and then subtracted it from my paycheck. The remaining amount was astounding. My mouth hung open when I saw the total. If I didn't know better, I would have suspected money gremlins with crack addictions came out at night while I was sleeping and depleted my bank account because I spent enough on movie rentals and tickets, magazines and books, coffee, and fast food to fund an African village. A large one. So Thoreau had been right. I could do with a lot less. A *lot* less.

I took a deep breath. I knew what I had to do because I knew me. The only way to break my consumer dependency was to cut off my supply line, money. I was the master of the impulse buy. If I could convince myself that I might need so much as a single line from a book, I would buy it. Although I wasn't nearly as bad as I had been in my youth, there was still a handful of bands whose new releases I'd mandated as automatic purchases. Approximately 80 percent of my movie collection was bought because I'd liked a film after having rented it, only to have my copy remain unwatched years later. Knowing all this, I started drafting my resignation. I then did something that, if the me of five or even two years prior had caught me doing, he would have snatched the pen I held in my hand and committed hara-kiri on the spot: I called the nearest state park, the same park that had almost taken my life as well as my wife's years before, and asked if Fraggle Fern's job was still available. He had recently quit in order to go back to school.

This was not the product of a midlife crisis or a psychotic breakdown. Thoreau had been right so far and I was curious what the completed picture looked like. There were other immediate advantages to a position as a trail maintenance worker. Much like people who work overtime in order to collect vacation days for when they are too tired to go to the office, I found it fascinating that individuals did the same in order to afford gym membership whenever they could step outside and take a walk or do push-ups for free. If I were to get a job roaming around in the woods, I would automatically improve my quality of life because I'd be getting paid to exercise. I looked forward to the prospect of fresh air as my eyes slowly recovered from reading obligatory journals under florescent lighting. Though my palms started to sweat at the mere thought, I even stood a good chance of experiencing what I now understood to be the thrill of seeing a real, live venomous snake. I continued tallying all the advantages while ignoring what I knew all-too-well were the disadvantages. I asked myself, *How bad could it be?* In the end, I wanted to know if I could find myself, even if I had to die in the process.

If I did get eaten by a badger, perhaps someone would write a book about me that might spur a Galtonian debate and my colleagues could discuss with students whether my untimely demise was the result of inferior breeding or poor upbringing. Regardless, I would undoubtedly be placed alongside Christopher McCandless as a prime example of the influential power of literature. He had set off into the Alaskan wilds due, in part, to Jack London's relayed adventures while in the frosty bush. McCandless died there at the age of 24 as a consequence of minimal preparation and very little wilderness knowledge. His tale was made famous by Jon Krakauer, whose 1996 best-seller, *Into the Wild*, was transformed into an Oscar-nominated film in 2007. If this was to be my fate, I didn't mind because I knew there were worse ways to die other than keeling over from what would essentially be a Thoreauvian overdose.

So I called the park. A female answered the phone. With the same chipper, unbridled, completely uncalled for enthusiasm as the state park employee years before—after being graciously thanked for my interest in the glorious wonders the natural world provided—I was told the position was still open and to "come on out" and apply. Forty-five minutes later, I was freshly reacquainted with the park's history when I hung up the phone just as my wife came home from work.

Oh boy, I thought, *now for the hard part.*

I asked her to join me at the kitchen table. She raised an eyebrow, walked into the kitchen, and leveraged her hand firmly on the back of a chair, thereby indicating she'd had a long day and wanted me to be swift with whatever bad news I had to relay. For some odd reason Francis Macomber's cause of death suddenly came to mind. His wife had "accidentally" shot him in the head.

I shrugged off the literary brain fart and informed my lovely bride I had chosen to relegate us to a life of perpetual poverty. After much consequential clawing and gnashing of teeth and her issuing me a complementary flesh wound which I hoped wouldn't leave too noticeable of a scar, she consented. She finally admitted that my newly chosen vocation would be a good change of pace for me. I think she relented after realizing that within a matter of months, or possibly even a few weeks, she could begin dating again after an officer stood on our doorstep and informed her that her husband, preoccupied with finding himself, had failed to watch where he'd been going and subsequently tripped over a grizzly which had been trying to sleep off a migraine. I wondered if it was legal for her to take out a life insurance policy on me without my signature.

My wife accompanied me to the state park the following evening. A lonely, beat-up car sat in the parking lot. Its only distinctive feature was a cracked and faded bumper sticker that read, "SUBURBIA: Where they cut down all the trees and name streets after them." Dressed in slacks and a button-up, *sans* tie so as to look more casual, I nervously entered a vacant visitor center.

As soon as I opened the door, we were accosted by a recording of bird song and the faint rattle of a relentless string of keystrokes, both of which echoed cavernously through the building, a building whose walls were apparently allergic to paint. There was an unhealthy surplus of wood grain everywhere. At first I wondered if the visitor center was in the process of being remodeled before humoring the possibility that the lack of finishing touches or even the remotest hint of interior design might be deliberate. I desperately searched for one civil surface with color other than brown, but my exploration ended in vain when it culminated at the building's apex, where a skylight had been installed. I couldn't figure out what purpose this ultimately served since roofs were made to keep the outside *out*. It was apparent this hadn't been the architect's intention because the floor was semi-polished stone, which amplified the birds' endless chirps and twitters and emphasized the fact that an innocent keyboard was being tortured somewhere nearby. Having simply erected four walls around a small parcel of the forest before going about their day, the building's designer and contractor had laughed amongst themselves all the way to the bank. But I forced myself to realign my cynical attitude. I was starting life afresh and, alas, the sun being cast through the misplaced window was shining biblically down upon me as if I were the Chosen One. I quickly abandoned this optimistic notion once I noticed my wife was also bathed in bright sunlight. It was then that I became aware either the keyboard had finally shuffled off its plastic coil or its abuser had succumbed to carpal tunnel. A few seconds later, a head peeped around a far corner. A short, bespectacled brunette who could have been Janeane Garofalo's stunt double walked over to us.

"Hey there. I thought I heard someone come in. You Mike?" the woman asked while extending a hand. She was wearing a forest green polo, beige slacks, and hiking boots and introduced herself as the park director. After graciously telling my wife to have a look around, she escorted me to her office. I thought I caught a whiff of pinecones as she turned and led the way.

She sat me down at a desk next to hers. Above us, like overgrown snowflakes suspended in midair, months of pages from a quote-a-day nature calendar had been taped to the ceiling. The director darted back and forth from one filing cabinet to the next, mumbling to herself as she yanked one sheet of paper after another from various manila folders. Each time she slammed a cabinet drawer, the quotes suddenly awoke in unified protest before gradually returning to their complacent, collective slumber. A framed diploma leaned against a two-tier letter tray on her desk. B.S. in Biology. A stuffed, portly, bucktoothed beaver guarded her degree from a nearby windowsill, which was otherwise populated by a colony of plastic toy lizards. The dust which had accumulated over the years made the chubby, flat-tailed mammal's black, marble eyes appear as if it had cataracts. A large blackbird was perched on a petrified branch above me and, next to it, a coiled copperhead.

I wondered how one would go about sport hunting a slithering reptile. Perhaps already at ease because I was in the process of leaving my trinket and stress-filled life behind, I started daydreaming. I visualized a dusty, desolate frontier town. As dried tumbleweed bumbled down the middle of the road that divided the makeshift settlement, a bandit with a bandana veiling the lower half of his face had his six-shooter drawn. A small snake stood erect before him at full surrender, quivering with fear. I inadvertently chuckled, which brought me back to the present moment. I looked over at the director. Busy ransacking another filing cabinet, she had failed to notice my indiscretion. I continued my survey of the room. A shadowbox full of crucified wasps hung next to a poster depicting a deer that seemed to be reading a NO HUNTING sign. At the foot of the director's desk, a bobcat perpetually pawed passersby. I surmised that unlike people with literature degrees, it appeared as if biologists preferred keeping their dead animals out in the open. Either that or I had inadvertently entered a museum depicting Noah's ark.

The director walked over, placed a bureaucratic stack of papers before me, and told me to begin filling them out. She then sat down at her desk and started frantically typing. As I completed one form after another after another — noting the irony of having to kill a tree in order to work in a forest — in one and the same motion, the keyboard went silent and the director swiveled around in her desk chair, deftly pushed off with her right foot, and effortlessly sailed over to me. She came to an eloquent halt at, if I had stopped to measure, what I was sure was exactly 18 inches.

Had I been caught? Did she somehow know that I had no business being in the woods, harbored a checkered past with the park, and no socially acceptable reason for wanting to work in the forest?

"So, what made you wanna work for a state park?"

She sat staring at me with a smile that mocked my guilt. I was tiptoeing along a razor's edge.

I paused, unsure if I should offer her the unbelievable truth — I was a multiple-degree holder with a cushy job that I was willfully throwing away for a minimum wage position which I knew might very well be the death of me because I wanted to "find myself" based on something I'd read about in an old book by a guy whose name no one could pronounce properly — or simply lie and say I was tired of flipping burgers. I decided that if I was going to make a clean break and start over, it should at least be an honest one.

"I wanna get out of the office," I told her. "Get some exercise."

"Oh yeah?" the director said. "Well, you'll definitely get that." I could tell by her inflection what she was about to ask. "Where you workin' these days?"

I paused.

"At the university." I left it at that.

"Oh yeah? Where *at* at the university?"

I grimaced.

"The English department," I mumbled.

"Oh yeah? What do you do there?"

Did, I thought to myself. I now saw that I had been a tad overzealous, having emailed my resignation to the chair that morning. Damn. How the director responded to my answer would determine whether I would be filing for unemployment the following day.

This was the moment of truth—or untruth. My mind raced between "teacher" and "custodian." I could feel stomach acid making its way up my esophagus.

"I . . . teach." My response had sounded almost like a question.

"Cool," she said while simultaneously swiveling back around and propelling herself back to her desk before summarily returning to work.

I sat there looking at the back of her head, unsure if it was the end of the conversation or the end of my trying to get a job there. Once she began pecking away at her keyboard, I shrugged and returned to my bottomless ream of application forms.

Having been trained in the Arts, I had never spent any quantifiable time with scientists, biologists or otherwise. I was unsure whether the director's happy-go-lucky demeanor was a personality quirk, the byproduct of the academic environment in which she had been reared, or the consequence of being a hippie. I thought to myself that if this was indeed her character, she was so laid back, she ran the risk of accidentally slipping into a coma at any minute.

After what seemed like hours later, as I tried to flex feeling back into my hand, I told the director I was done filling out the paperwork.

"Oh yeah? We'll just see about that," she said.

I was confused and slightly terrified. Her tone was playful but left room for her intent to mean she was about to snatch the papers I was holding out to her, toss them in the trash, and point to the door.

She took the stack and, as if quickly assessing an exam to estimate whether I might have passed, glanced at the first application form, flipped to the one behind it and skimmed its contents, before proceeding to the next. During this time, the urge to pee became overwhelming.

"Not bad," she finally said after finishing the last page and, with an adroit flick of the wrist, flopped my employment dossier back to the front. "Nine times out of ten people miss a few questions. Looks like you got them all. Okay, I'll get these sent off to HQ. Should be a coupla days. I'll call you."

After thanking her for her time, I walked over to the restroom as casually as possible, hoping all the while the director didn't notice I was taking baby steps, and reveled in one of the more enjoyable urinations of my life. Though I highly doubted Thoreau did so, because one of the underlying themes of his philosophy is to be mindful of our physical selves, I rated my bathroom experience an 8 out of a possible 10. Its high score was undoubtedly due to the physical release of career-changing tension and anxiety. When I opened the bathroom door, I was greeted by my grinning wife.

She dropped her head and whispered "I like her" as we left the building.

"How? You two didn't even say anything to each other except 'Hi.'"

"I know, but I caught bits and pieces of what you two were saying. Between the bird calls."

"Figures."

"What? Why?"

"It felt like a rainbow gathering in there with you two," I chided as I casually stepped an elbow jab's distance away.

She just smiled and waited until I came back within range before landing a solid blow to my ribcage.

Feigning injury, I asked, "You think I got the job?" I was fearful of the implications of being overqualified since it was a non-degreed position.

"Stop it," she insisted as she peered down where I was massaging my side for playful emphasis. "That didn't hurt," she declared before announcing, "Yes, you got the job" with an exasperated sigh, as if I'd asked a silly question.

As I anxiously awaited the employment verdict, I started to put Thoreau's principle of simple living into practice: "Before we can adorn our houses with beautiful objects the walls must be stripped, and our lives must be stripped, and beautiful housekeeping and beautiful living be laid for a foundation . . . ." I placed a notice in the paper advertising a yard sale the following weekend. Despite it being the onset of winter, I went on to sell all but 20 of my 2,000 volumes. I erected grossly askew clothesline poles, which made my eco-wife extremely happy, so much so that I wasn't obligated to do the dishes for an entire week. Three days after meeting with the park director, largely to distract myself from the fact that she had yet to call, I begun turning over a small plot of earth in the backyard for a spring garden. As I stared blankly at a clod of dirt which rested in the head of my shovel and dwelt upon what the remainder of my life might be like, my wife yelled my name from the front of the house.

I dropped the shovel, dashed up the porch steps, and burst through the back door, which lead directly into the kitchen. There my wife stood, calmly cooking. I had expected her to be holding the phone. Confused and slightly unnerved, I asked her what she needed.

She flipped the spatula she was holding upright to keep the oil from dripping on the floor, turned to me, and said, "The park called."

Her deadpan tone was indecipherable in its indifference.

"And?" I fretfully blurted out.

"You got the job. You start on Monday."

I exhaled. I hadn't realized I'd not taken a breath since slinging open the back door.

Then it occurred to me. I knew nothing about trail maintenance. I shrugged. *How hard could a minimum wage job be?* I thought to myself. Besides, I had broader, more philosophical issues which I needed to begin preparing to address because, as Thoreau went on to add, ". . . a taste for the beautiful is most cultivated out of doors, where there is no house and no housekeeper."

Thoreau had been wrong about one thing. I was now Nature's Housekeeper.

Chapter 5

Stalking the Elusive Missouri Tree Snorer

I soon discovered that, again, Thoreau had been right. There was no house in the middle of the woods, no less a heated home with a bathroom. Anxious to begin finding myself, I decided to go out to the park and get acquainted with its shortest trail before my official start date rolled around. I asked my wife if she'd like to accompany me.

"No," she politely, but stalwartly, replied. "Think I'll stick with just *liking* the idea of nature." To this day, she has never returned to the woods, yet somehow this new venture of mine had returned us to being in sync as a stable, albeit atypical, couple.

Having printed a map of the park off the Internet, I now saw that the senior citizen trail resided *behind* the visitor center. As for the other trails, even though I had traversed two of them already, they remained squiggly lines on the page amid a spaghetti pile of roads throughout the park.

I drove to my new place of employment, turned at its entrance, and slowly crept down the road to the visitor center. I took a deep breath and tried to appreciate the barren trees that surrounded me on all sides. As I watched one gray-brown overgrown twig after another pass by my window, I optimistically turned my attention to the next hoping to see something a little more interesting. I was met by more gray-brown sticks. Just as boredom started setting in, the visitor center's parking lot came into view.

It was vacant. This alarmed me because I expected it to be full of vehicles with Sierra Club window magnets and bumper stickers that read "Save the Whales!" I looked to see if the pavement reached around the building, thinking that perhaps all of my fellow nature lovers had chosen to park closer to the trailhead. It did not. I shrugged off this anomaly as the consequence of a local football game and the holiday season.

Having learned from Thoreau that one of the beauties of nature is its sound, I quickly got out of my car and listened. Although a slight, chilling wind rudely snatched the residual warmth left by the car's heater from me, I heard nothing. I looked up at the tree tops, expecting to see songbirds, only to find that they were empty because the feathered vocalists were apparently on lunch break. Then, suddenly, a prolonged creaking shattered the silence. It was as if someone had slowly opened a door with rusty hinges. I scanned the immediate vicinity, trying to trace the source of the unnatural sound. I saw no one. I then realized I was getting a little cold.

I put on a sweater, hoodie, and my coat. Before I got dressed that morning, I had slipped into the "job-warming" gift my wife had given me—a bright red, insulated, adult-sized onesie, complete with butt flap. I felt remotely hippie because I was also wearing new wool socks. However, they were conveniently hidden under my own job-warming gift to myself: a new pair of hiking boots. I donned my scarf, beanie, and shimmied mittens down over my gloves. I had left my knitted ski mask at home because I thought it might be a bit much, but hoped I wouldn't regret it. Because I was now a professional trail maintenance worker, I was no longer anyone's nature fool. I had bookmarked the local weather on my computer for daily review. It was a frigid 57 degrees outside. I double-checked to make sure the almonds and park map I had placed in my coat pocket before leaving the house were where I'd left them and then, like a veteran hiker, grabbed my two bottles of water. I was ready to begin being a nature lover.

I started down the boardwalk that ran alongside the visitor center. Sure enough, it wrapped itself around the back of the building before extending out into the woods. Less than 30 feet from the visitor center's rear entrance, the walkway ended. I gleefully stepped onto actual dirt. I took a deep breath and slowly exhaled: I was now a part of nature. Twenty yards later, I came to a fork. I didn't remember a junction being on the map. I began to get worried, thinking I had already gotten lost. I plunged my over-padded hand into my coat pocket and yanked out my map. I uttered a sigh of relief. Thankfully, the trail split just after its commencement. As directed, I went left and ascended a slight incline that opened the senior citizen trail.

I heard the prolonged creaking again. It had come from nowhere. I looked around. Nothing. After another second's pause, I decided to keep forging ahead.

The first thing I realized about my new mindset toward nature was that the air of freedom eased the weight of walking. Like any task, the chore of hiking ceased to be a burden once I convinced myself that I wanted to do it. The next thing I noticed was that my boots were very, very stiff. I ignored the slight irritation and contentedly made my way along the pathway. I looked around. All the foliage was gone from everything except one type of medium-sized, scraggly tree. I tried to remember the name of the plant from biology class. The leaf's shape looked familiar, but I could not recall what it was. I blissfully dismissed my ignorance. I would have the rest of my life to figure out its name, average height, geographic range, preferred soil conditions, and the bugs it harbored. I continued happily down the trail.

After a short while I realized I was a little warm. I brushed this peevish annoyance aside because I'd just scaled a sizable hill. Five minutes later streams of perspiration began dribbling down my face. I could not reconcile why I was sweating in 57-degree weather. It was winter. Winter was cold. People didn't sweat when it was cold. They perspired in summer when it was hot. Regardless of the incongruity, I started removing layers.

As I attempted to figure out how I was going to carry my folded, yet still cumbersome, coat and hoodie—while making a mental note to bring my college backpack with me from now on for just such occasions—a sudden, very loud noise broke to my left. I instinctively turned, but my knees were bent in the opposite direction and I was prepared to run. Three deer stood approximately 50 feet from me. I had never seen deer before. I stared at them and they stared curiously back. I watched as they tilted their ears in one direction and then the next like little satellites attempting to pick up a signal. The moisture on their noses glistened in the overcast sunlight. After several magical seconds, one spooked for no explicable reason. They all darted off into the woods. Without thinking, I ran after them. It was only after they disappeared over a hill that it occurred to me what I'd done. I had left the trail. I turned around and sprinted back before someone had a chance to notice my impulsive, park-violating indiscretion.

Safely within the trail's confines once more, I felt my first official wilderness hunger pang. Proud I'd prepared for such a contingency, I got out my lunch. I stood there, in the middle of the forest, basking in the euphoric silence and solitude, and visualized the trio of deer as I nibbled on my almonds. One fell to the ground. I looked at it, unsure what to do. I vaguely remembered something my wife had said about leaving no footprint when in nature, but I was conflicted. I didn't want a dirty almond in my pocket and knew squirrels liked nuts. I liked squirrels. Although I was aware they had already stored food for the winter, I reasoned that they might be appreciative if I left some out in the event they ran a little short before spring. Once I got my fill, I carefully poured the remainder of my meal into a neat little pile. I brushed aside the autumn leaves to make it easier for my fuzzy friends to find my gift. Satisfied that I had done a good deed and helped nature, I continued down the trail.

The rusty hinge creaked again. After darting my head to the left and then the right in the vain attempt at catching the culprit at work, I began to get paranoid. I stood still, only moving my eyes back and forth so as not to betray my position. As I did this, I became fleetingly aware that the top of my big toe felt warm, almost hot, before conceiving of squinting so as to better scrutinize the nearby hills. Frustratingly, nothing moved. Several minutes later, I apprehensively started walking.

Not long after, I realized I had been in the woods for what seemed to have been quite some time. As I took another drink and mindlessly rubbed the back of my Achilles tendon, I got out my map and looked to make sure the trail was half a mile. It was. I then noticed my water bottle was empty. I found this peculiar since, again, it was the middle of winter and people don't get thirsty unless it is hot. I then had the sudden urge to pee. I looked around, careful to listen for the rustling of leaves underfoot. Hearing nothing, I unzipped. Although my urination of a few days prior had been one for the record books, this one automatically became a Top 3 contender, a near perfect 10. As I stood writing my name in the middle of the pathway and unrepentantly flashed the forest, numerous years of classroom stress trickled down the trail.

I was suddenly cold again. I re-layered while recalling the parable of Goldilocks and the Three Bears. I couldn't seem to get my temperature "just right." Merely regulating my body heat in the wild was exhausting. As I wrapped my scarf around my neck, the creaking started again.

This time it mocked me. The noise doubled its duration, but I was still unable to locate its source. Scared, I called out. Nothing. I had hoped that whoever was perpetrating the gag would show themselves after I'd admitted they'd bested me. Yet no one did. I stood there, waiting until they moved just a fraction of an inch. I was met by dead silence. Then it occurred to me: I had no idea what sound deer made. I quickly deduced that the squawking had very likely been the trio of satellite ears talking to one another. I chuckled to myself at the thought of having been spooked by Bambi.

Approximately an hour after I'd started, I emerged from the forest. Unlike my previous hikes, I was not elated at the sight of the boardwalk once it presented itself. I had enjoyed my time in the wilderness because, as Thoreau had observed, I knew it to be home. As I drove away, I noticed my shoulders felt better and seemed to hang lower. I had decompressed because I knew I'd made the right choice.

When I got home, I learned a valuable, hard-won lesson I dubbed the three B's: boots, blisters, and bathwater. As soon as I walked through the door, I shed my top layers as I ran a warm, soothing, relaxing bath. When I made it down to my socks, they didn't slide off. Instead, I had to slowly, gently separate the now encrusted wool from seeping, open blisters. After I removed both socks, I looked at my feet, which appeared to be leprous. I then naively stepped into the steaming hot water. My wife came rushing in shortly thereafter.

"What? What was that scream?" she asked as she looked around the bathroom trying to find me. "Are you alright?" she added, once she'd found me sitting in the tub.

"Yeah," I said with a throaty grimace as I tried to suppress the tears that were ardently trying to break free from my eyes. "Fine," I grumbled. "Just a little sore."

After I refused to elaborate, she disappeared into the house while half-mocking, half-proudly mumbling, "That's my Grizzly Adams." Once the burning, searing pain in my feet began to subside, I reflected back on my day. Despite my blisters, I was surprised to realize that I actually looked forward to my time in the woods because I was sure that everything was going to be alright.

Everything was not alright. I had not made the right choice. I was sitting approximately 15 feet above the very hard, very cold ground. I was sweating profusely even though my body heat was slowly melting the 3-inch-thick sheet of ice beneath me. I had lost all feeling in my hands, not from the petrifying temperature, but the incessant vibration. After three hours of non-stop work, I had progressed exactly zero feet down the trail.

The day after I had taken my inaugural trail maintenance hike, a catastrophic winter storm started making its way across the United States. A few days later, it hit the region. Half the city was without power for over a week. Homes burned after novice fireplace owners got slaphappy with their fuel and the overburdened fire department couldn't make it up glazed, icy hills in time. The park was forced to close for the first time in its history. A rough survey suggested that the trails averaged a downed tree every 500 feet. The park houses 18 miles of nature walkways. Without having any way of knowing for sure, it was possible that over 200 trees blocked the footpaths. Two weeks later, the roads were finally clear as the Red Cross packed what little supplies it had left after going door-to-door helping the stranded, frozen citizens, many of whom had never experienced an ice storm during their lifetime, much less one of such crippling magnitude and ferocity.

The park director had called me the day before and asked if the roads in front of my house were open. I told her I could make it out. Since my formal training was *supposed* to have started two weeks prior, I was unsure what to bring with me. I didn't know how to use a chainsaw and the only tool I possessed which I thought might be of use was a hatchet that had been left to me by the previous homeowner. The typical 20-minute drive to the park took a solid hour.

Once there, I was met by equal parts winter wonderland and apocalyptic terror. I shivered outside the visitor center in speechless amazement. Ice hung from every conceivable surface. Icicles twinkled each time the face-numbing wind blew, initiating a symphony of angelic chimes and miniature bells. The enchanted music was juxtaposed by the harsh, cacophonous, unrelenting noise of multiple chainsaws off in the distance, which sounded like a horde of premenstrual bumblebees had descended upon the forest. As I stood there, taking it all in, the director came out and greeted me.

"Well, look at it this way," she said. "After this, everything you do out here will be a walk in the park."

I looked at her, smirking at the stillborn pun.

"Well, uh, what would you like me to do?" I asked.

"From the size of things, it really doesn't matter. Given where we are at this point, every little bit helps," she informed me.

Not knowing what this meant exactly, I said, "I brought a hatchet. Will that work?"

"Does it chop?" she sarcastically inquired.

Taking her at face value, I was taken aback by the implication that some hatchets apparently did not do what they were designed to. I quickly estimated whether mine was in working condition. Still somewhat confused, I meekly said, "Yeah, I guess."

"Well then, get started whacking some trees," she enthusiastically instructed as she jutted a mittened thumb back behind the visitor center.

I suited up, strapped on my backpack full of water and food, and headed to the senior citizen trail. Perhaps the director already knew this, but—due to no lack of effort on my part—a "little bit" is the exact amount of assistance I would provide the park during my first few days as a trail maintenance worker. My fear of being overqualified was unfounded; I quickly discovered that I was vastly *under*qualified to do a minimum wage job.

I met my first downed tree no more than six feet off the boardwalk. It had fallen alongside and parallel to the trail and its crown blocked the path. I quickly set to work. Deciding it was best to start at the top, I carefully scaled the horizontal giant. Each time there was a strong gust of wind, the ice that clung to the tops of the trees that had been loosened by the early morning sun rained down on me like wet, shattered glass. I had never chopped wood before and though I made progress by diligently hammering away on the smaller branches, I quickly realized it was unreasonable to try to cut through anything thicker than my thigh. Once I'd reached complete exhaustion, I made my descent and returned to the visitor center. I only had enough energy to tell the director I'd be back the next day.

When I arrived the following blisteringly chilly morning, I walked into the visitor center to fill my water bottles. The director came up to me and smiled. Try as I might, I could not hide the look of utter defeat that had set in the day before.

"Good news," she said. "We've got some people who used to work for the B.L.M. coming out for a day. They'll be here next week sometime. Purple isn't as bad as I thought it was gonna be, but I'm kinda worried about Pond."

I stared at her, clueless. Academia has business acronyms, but they were fairly sporadic and context clues usually gives one a fighting chance at what they mean. I now felt as if I'd missed the opening week of basic training.

"What's the B.L. . . . ?" I stopped short. I didn't want to add "T" but, in my epic confusion, couldn't remember the last letter.

"B.L.M. Bureau of Land Management. A couple who used to work for them out West called and asked if they could come out with some friends and help. I said, 'Why not?' You should go with them, you might learn something. They'll be crosscutting."

I stood there, dumbfounded. She had answered my question using more terms I didn't understand. I failed to comprehend how watching people cut sideways through a log constituted a learning experience. I had surmised that purple not being as bad as she'd anticipated was a good thing, but not knowing how a color might suffer from an ice storm, I couldn't say for sure, anymore than I knew why she'd be worried about a pond given the circumstances. It took me quite some time to get a handle on her bio-trail-speak.

I elected to nod politely instead of making a bigger fool of myself.

"You still want me to go out then?"

She looked at me and grinned. Her smile was equal parts restrained laugher and pity.

"Sure, knock yourself out."

I spent another anguishing day doggedly beating the hell out of a tree in subfreezing temperatures. I could barely lift my arm above my head due to the stiffness which had set in the night before. As a result, my pace — and therefore my morale — dropped considerably. After half an hour's bludgeoning, I stepped back to review my progress. I'd made it halfway through a branch that was no bigger than my arm. I might as well have been tickling the tree with a feather.

By the time twilight began to bleed into the early winter night, largely out of sheer will, I had somehow removed every branch I could from the crown. What was left would have to be cut with a chainsaw. I packed up and, dripping with sweat even though I had stripped down to a t-shirt, ambled back to my car and drove away.

When I got home, I took the charcoal portrait of Thoreau that I had done a year before which sat proudly on my desk and put it facedown in a drawer. That weekend I slept more soundly than I had in my entire life.

When I arrived to work on Monday morning, the director called me into her office. I knew that I was being fired. She had undoubtedly stepped outside the back door of the visitor center and noticed how little progress I'd made over two days.

"So whaddya think so far?" she asked as we both sat down.

I paused. Did I feign enjoying the toils which had put me in a near 48-hour coma or did I tell her the truth, therefore placing unnecessary doubt in her mind as to my ability and willingness to do the job?

The truth had worked before.

"Oh, it's great," I blurted out before pausing to contemplate my lie. My guilt got the best of me. I reluctantly admitted, "But I don't feel like I did all that much. I hacked away at that tree for two days and didn't make so much as a dent."

She smiled and leaned over to her desk. She turned back around and handed me an intimidating pile of manuals and VHS tapes. At its base was a very thick textbook.

"Here. Flip through these and watch some of the videos."

I looked down at what she'd handed me. A film titled "An Ax to Grind" rested on top. I tilted the stack sideways so I could read the spines. There were introductory materials on crosscut saws, trail maintenance tools and equipment, blade sharpening, trail construction, and *Lightly on the Land*, a 267-page trail maintenance encyclopedia.

I looked up at her.

"Take 'em home and watch 'em. Go play around in the tool shed tomorrow. Check out what we've got out there." She swiveled around in her chair and started typing.

I wasn't sure what she wanted me to do. Was she sending me home for the day to do my assigned homework? I got up, but before I made it out of the room, I turned back around.

"Three questions," I said.

She swiveled to face me.

"What's up?"

"So you want me to go home and go through these?"

"Yep."

"Two, where's the tool shed?"

I was quietly proud of myself; I had asked for directions.

My moment of glory quickly subsided. The director gave me a look of playfully haughty derision. I'd obviously asked a stupid question. I figured the answer was as simple as looking at a park map.

"Okay. Three, I was out here a couple of weeks ago and out on the senior citizen trail I kept hearing a creaking like someone was opening a door with really rusty hinges. Is that a deer? What is that?"

Without so much as a pause, she replied, "Oh . . . *yeah* . . . . No. Those aren't deer. There's a lot of Missouri tree snorers on SCT."

Not surprised that I'd never heard the name, I was simply happy that I had gotten an answer I could somewhat understand—and a decipherable acronym to boot. I shrugged and went to my car.

Shortly after I arrived home, I discovered one very important fact.

Just because you have a college degree doesn't mean you know everything. A higher ed diploma merely allows a person to understand a particular subject a little more easily. No more, no less. A testament to this hard truth would hit shelves a few years later, Matthew Crawford's *Shop Class as Soulcraft: An Inquiry into the Value of Work*. If I would have read his writing while I was still a teacher, I would have dismissed the author's central idea— that the manual trades frequently demand as much, if not more, critical thought than what a professor does in a classroom or a researcher in a lab—as the byproduct of a guy with a doctorate who was crying sour grapes after being denied tenure. However, I would live Crawford's thesis long before he started penning the book.

For example, chopping a log in half can be done one of two ways. The frustratingly, grossly ineffective way that takes forever, a.k.a. my way, or the right, extremely eloquent way, which is an art form. The time-proven, proper means of going about chopping a log in half begins by starting a cut and then measuring the log's diameter and creating another at that approximate length. To make a cut, your blade needs to land at a 22 to 45-degree angle. After the first stroke, you then strike from the opposite direction from the same angle, thereby completing a 44 to 90-degree cut. This is why you see professional lumberjacks hopping back and forth over a log. Instead of trying to contort your wrist into bending at an unnatural counterangle, it is easier to just step over the tree. If you're lucky, a cute little wedge will come flying out. As you work one side and then the other, the gap will slowly narrow as you make your way through the timber. If you measured your initial distance properly, your final stroke will be straight down as you slice through the bottom of a wide-mouthed, gaping V. The secret to chopping wood is, as with most tools, letting the ax do the work. If your blade is sharp enough, the weight of the ax head carries enough force to get through a log with little actual effort other than lifting the tool over your head.

And so it went. After learning my way around an ax, I decided to change pace and browse through a pamphlet titled, "Handtools for Trail Work," which housed diagrams and explanations of various trail maintenance equipment. I was already familiar with one, the folding saw, which Fraggle Fern had used to trim my nose hair. I knew what a machete was and had seen a weed whip in Stuart Rosenberg's 1967 film, *Cool Hand Luke*. In the classic tale about integrity, characters refer to weed whips as "yo-yos." It is a handled instrument whose yoke forms a Y which harbors a serrated bar at its mouth that grips and tears foliage. It gets its nickname from the pendulum-like motion it makes when chopping weeds. A Pulaski was new. It is part ax, part garden hoe used for cutting through exposed tree roots. A McLeod is a huge metal comb for smoothing out and setting tread. The trail term for long-handled pruning shears is "loppers."

My trail maintenance education was going well until I started boning up on how to put the various tools to work. In the *Trail Construction and Maintenance Notebook*, I discovered that the key to building a good wilderness pathway is largely dependent upon slopes, grades, and pitches, all of which must be carefully weighed and considered when designing, restoring, or rerouting a trail. I quickly deduced that in order to be proficient in this arena of trail maintenance, one must possess advanced degrees in engineering, soil science, geology, and hydrology. I had one too many literature diplomas, which meant I could read *really* fast, but rode the mathematical short bus. This was a problem. To set a grade, one must know geometry and a lot of it. Furthermore, until that moment, I had labored under the naïve notion that dirt was dirt. I was now expected to be able to differentiate between *silt* and *peat*. To make matters worse, I would also have to consider the percentage of rock which sat on or near the ground's surface because its presence increases water distribution. If I couldn't estimate within a very narrow margin of error the strength and volume of water passing through a set area, the entire trail might wash away after the first heavy rain.

It seemed inevitable I would be embarrassingly fired from a minimum wage job because this was beyond my scope and range. I had entered the woods with the ability to assess whether a landscape was aesthetically appealing, not solve complex differential equations. To lighten my spirits, I pushed aside the frighteningly thick *Lightly on the Land* and put in a video about blade sharpening. Within minutes, I was lulled into a warm, soporific trance as a man in a plaid wool shirt hypnotized me by rocking a file back and forth, to and fro, over an upturned ax. I was surprised that he pushed the file *into* the ax head instead of *away* from it because doing so seemed counterintuitive. However, after giving it a few seconds' thought, this made sense. The method is simple enough, but there is one trick: You have to keep your hand steady. In order to create a refined edge, the blacksmith has to make sure the file meets the blade at the exact same angle each and every time.

I was left with another film, the cryptically-titled "Crosscut Saw Training," or *Lightly on the Land*. I thought it best to get the worst over with and then celebrate with a movie. Although a few chapters covered what I'd already learned, my elevated spirits plummeted into a deep depression when, page-after-page, one foreign term was explained by another. Trail Maintenance didn't have its own vocabulary; it was its own language. I'd already been intimidated by "cribbing," "stabilizers," "outslopes," "backslopes," "tread," "turnpikes," "buffer zones," "backfill," and "water bars" when I was being morally and intellectually abused by slopes and grades. Now I had to deal with "hat racks," "slough," "blazing" versus "blazes," "switchbacks," "corridors," "duff," "berms," "puncheons," "flagging," and "blowdowns."

By the time I got to the chapter on crosscut saws, I realized there was yet another about how to use them. My wife told me dinner was ready. I glanced up at the clock: I had been studying all day. Using the notes I'd taken, she quizzed me as we ate. After we'd finished dessert, I made the decision that it'd be a better showing if I passed with high marks in most areas and outright failed in another than to barely pass all of them. I could then appeal to retake the botched exam and redeem my blemished academic reputation. I reviewed my notes and re-watched the videos. At midnight, no longer able to keep my eyes open, I looked over at my wife. She had fallen asleep while reading Tom Wolfe's *The Electric Kool-Aid Acid Test*.

I returned to the park the next day with a head full of semi-organized, solely theoretical knowledge. I walked into the visitor center and entered the director's office with pencil in-hand. She sat with her back to the door, typing as usual.

I continued standing in the doorway, waiting for her to notice me.

After several minutes, fearful I would lose control and begin confusing the barely contained terms and definitions bouncing around in my brain, I gingerly cleared my throat.

She swiveled around in her chair.

"What's up?"

I smiled, giving her time to remember that I had to take my tests. She smiled back, waiting for me to answer her question.

"I read what you gave me and watched the videos," I informed her, hoping this would serve as a polite reminder of what I needed to do that day. I thought it best to postpone mentioning that I'd deliberately skipped an entire unit.

"Oh yeah? So, whaddya think?"

Unprepared to give a presentation upon the material, regardless of how informal, I stood there, speechless. The director patiently awaited my response.

Out of sheer nervousness, I blurted out, "I didn't have time to watch the crosscut video."

I knew the insubordination citation prefacing my immediate dismissal was seconds away.

"Well, I would say not to worry because that's why I was going to have you head out with the B.L.M. gang, but they showed up early after you left yesterday. I thought they'd be here for three or four days, but they got through everything in the park. I couldn't believe it. Between them and the chainsaws, we're good to go. No biggie. I was planning on sending you up to do a crosscut workshop in a month or so anyway."

Again, I wasn't sure what this meant, but got the impression I'd somehow dodged a bullet. Not knowing what to say next, I stood there awkwardly awaiting direction.

Sensing my confusion, the director asked, "So'd you look over the other stuff I gave you?"

I was now in a perpetual state of bewilderment because the question implied she wouldn't have been disappointed if I said I had not, even though she'd sent me home to do just that.

"Yep," I proudly reported. The testing was about to begin.

"Good. Head off to the tool shed and fiddle around out there a bit. Then, I guess, go over to Blue and start clearing some berms outta the way."

With that, she swiveled back around and returned to work.

I knew all too well that most students would have been ecstatic at the announcement of an exam's cancelation, but being a life-long academe, I felt lost. However, I soon discovered I had not been issued a get-out-of-test-free card. My exam was going to be a self-evaluation that would take place in the field or, rather, the forest. I failed miserably.

I left the visitor center and got in my car. I slung open *Lightly on the Land* to review what a "berm" was. A *berm* is a collection of debris that obstructs the trail and redirects water flow. This is a bad thing because it invites Murphy's Law. A berm almost always pushes water where you don't want it. If it channels rain down the center of a trail, the walkway remains drenched, becomes slippery, and is more prone to erosion. If it runs perpendicular, the runoff will gradually chew out a small ditch in the middle of the pathway which will, over time, open into a yawning chasm. Berms typically appear after heavy rains when a branch hangs up on a trail and leaves collect behind it.

As I reviewed what constituted a berm, I thought to myself that a rake should suffice because that is what people use to get rid of sticks and leaves. It then occurred to me that my job was glorified yard work. I didn't mind. My newly-minted career aided hikers and other nature lovers as well as helped the wilderness itself. I reminded myself that I was now Nature's Housekeeper. There was only one problem or, to be concise, two: I didn't know where to find my broom closet or what "Blue" was.

Given the context, I presumed Blue was the name of a trail, but looking at my park map, I could find neither it *nor* the tool shed. I returned to the map's key time and again. There was no "TS," "B," or "Blue" listed. There was no tiny symbol of an ax or a saw. I did manage to locate several bathrooms on the park grounds, which I considered hiding in, but quickly decided against since I was fairly certain the berms wouldn't go away on their own.

Determined not to let such a minor inconvenience as trying to find a 12 x 12-foot building in the middle of 3,000 acres worry me, I assumed the role of a chipper, upbeat naturephiliac who was now in the place he so dearly loved. I forced myself to view this as an opportunity to familiarize myself with my workplace. I got in my car and drove into the heart of the park.

Hours later I was running low on gas. I had repeatedly passed a pond, which I deduced was what the director had referenced the day before as being a concern since a trailhead was marked at its entrance. The start of the trail was complemented by numerous sharp, chiseled trunk spears crafted by beavers, which I mentally assigned No. 76 in the various ways I might die in the woods once I lost my footing on the slippery, berm-lined pathway and became a human shish kabob. During my charter park voyage, I had also met countless outhouses, kiosks with lonely picnic tables beneath them, campgrounds, one sign after another designating a multitude of trails—although never one that read "Blue Trail"—or anything that could be mistaken for a tool shed. By the time I admitted defeat and returned to the visitor center, I assumed I had seen every part of the park except the two that I needed.

Nervously, I entered the director's office.

"What's up?" she asked, before glancing at her watch. "Don't tell me you already have all the berms cleared off the trail." In my steadfast stupidity, I didn't know that this was a joke in-and-of itself because Blue ran a full six miles.

I decided that I had given her enough reason to doubt me over the last few days. I opted to try to distract her with comedy.

"I have driven all over the place and apparently someone moved the tool shed."

Without so much as a hint of irritation at my ignorance, she slung a thumb over her shoulder, "Back behind us. Can't miss it."

Because she'd managed to eradicate any semblance of pride with a single swipe of her hand, I went for broke.

"Okay. Where's Blue Trail?" I hoped I'd made the right assumption that the color was attached to a trail.

"Down the road, turn left, first trail on your right."

I stopped and thought a minute. I had passed by that way at least nine times. The first marked trail on the right wasn't labeled "Blue."

My befuddlement being readily apparent, the director magically produced a park map of her own and started scribbling on it. Moments later she handed it to me. Over the various trails, she had written names: "Pond," "Purple," "Blue," "Orange," and "SCT." As I stared down at the map, realizing that the park employees had their own code names for the various pathways, I got a little queasy. I hoped that they didn't have generic terms for all the tools and maintenance techniques too, otherwise I would have to memorize twice as many technical definitions. I suspected my park nickname was "Dumbass."

I walked out the back entrance of the visitor center and was immediately met by a bright red tool shed. I couldn't believe my eyes. I had driven over a hundred miles and it had been sitting a few yards from where I had stood every day when I arrived at work. I had even passed by it on three separate occasions when working the SCT. How had I missed this? It was not only big, it was painted *bright red*. Not camouflage. Not even green. It was very, very red.

I opened the door only to discover I'd found trail maintenance heaven. I was surprised a choir of angels in hiking boots didn't start belting out Woody Guthrie's "This Land is Your Land" as soon as I stepped inside. A cornucopia of equipment, all neatly arranged, rested on the walls and shelves. It was as if the trail textbook I had been reading the day before had come to life. Multiple folding saws, axes, yo-yos, Pulaskis, McLeods, and loppers lined the room. Once my initial amazement wore off, I began looking for a garden rake. Because everything was astonishingly well organized, I was surprised when one didn't jump out at me. Finally, in the far corner, a single, barely used, orphaned rake leaned against the wall. I grabbed it, slung it over my shoulder and, like Huck Finn tramping down the Mississippi's banks, walked merrily to my car.

As with the tool shed, Blue Trail was exactly where the director said it was. Although the ice had begun to melt, the walkway was still slick in some areas and, I quickly realized, muddy in others. I entered the trail and every time a pile of leaves presented itself, I pulled it to the side. Shortly into the hike, I came to a small creek. It had been below freezing for most of the day, so I was surprised to find a trickle of water avidly running along its rock-lined bottom. As predicted, like an overgrown virus, a large ball of leaves with branches randomly protruding from its center had attached itself to the intersection of creek and trail. I slung my rake into the top of it. It didn't budge. I grabbed the rake handle with both hands and tugged. The nest of leaves broke apart. I pushed and pulled the smaller wads of debris into and down the miniature stream.

Then I froze. A creaking started to give way, which grew louder with each passing second. I chuckled at myself: It was only a Missouri tree snorer. Knowing I wouldn't be able to locate it, I nodded in recognition of my newfound wilderness knowledge and headed down the trail.

And so the day went. I took lunch outside, just like Thoreau, and listened to the tree snorers come and go. Not long after I packed everything up, seized my trusty rake, and went back to work, I came upon a rather large creek. I looked at my map. I stood up, proud. I had hiked an entire mile. I assessed the situation. The middle of the creek bed remained unobstructed because water was coursing through it at an alarming rate, but berms had accumulated along its borders. I slowly stepped into the glacial tide, which surged under curtains of icicles on either side of the eroded embankment. I plunged the rake into a sizable berm and, pulling with both hands, jerked backward. The apparently freeze-resistant, slimy algae, which adamantly clung to the rocks below my feet, combined with the flowing water to form a frictionless surface. It was as if someone had pulled a rug out from under me.

I fell backward and hit the rocks hard. I was instantly drenched. I thought to myself that the high today was only going to be 34 degrees.

Still unfamiliar with the intricacies of hypothermia, I nonetheless grabbed my backpack and the rake and started running down the trail. Removing berms did not generate nearly the same amount of body heat as chopping wood. A biting chill was already beginning to climb up my spine. As I ran, I could hear water sloshing in my boots with every step. It had yet to be determined whether my future communication with the shoe company would be in the form of a lawsuit based on frostbitten toes or a strongly worded letter informing the manufacturer that the terms "waterproof" and "sponge" were antonyms, not synonyms.

Eventually I saw my car in the distance. Although I had run non-stop, I was shivering by the time I made it to the trailhead. I had watched enough movies to know the dangers I faced if I remained in my soaked clothes. I stripped down and turned on the heater. After 20 minutes, the chills subsided. Once I believed myself to be out of the immediate danger of losing any extremities, I made the executive decision to go home. After I'd taken a hot shower, donned every article of clothing in my closet, and jacked the thermostat up to a pleasant 85 degrees, I would call the director and tell her I'd make up the lost hours over the weekend. I put the car in gear and started down the road.

As I drove toward the visitor center on my way out of the park, I did a double-take. The director was standing outside talking to a very prim, proper, official-looking individual. The official broke off in mid-conversation when the two of them turned to give a cursory glance at the passing car. I slinked down in the driver's seat and sheepishly waved.

To my chagrin, I could read the man's lips as he asked the director "Is that guy naked?" Both of them waved back in speechless, stunned amazement.

After I arrived home and got warm, I reluctantly dialed the phone. The director answered.

"So I guess you'd like to know what that was all about?" I said, without so much as a "Hello" beforehand. I could hear people laughing in the background.

"Well, yeah. Sorta. When I told you to go have fun in the forest, I didn't mean it *that* way."

Once I told her what had happened and she stopped giggling, the director instructed me to stay warm and, to my relief, said she'd see me the next day.

As soon as I opened the door to the visitor center the following morning, I heard laughter. At first I believed it was because I was taking labored micro steps because my thighs were epically sore from having run through the hills at a relentless, breakneck pace. Each stride felt as if I was wading through cooled, smelt metal. But I was greeted by the backs of a gaggle of forest green shirts which were gathered around the director's office. As I approached, one of the smiling malingerers who was leaning on the door frame noticed me. He nudged the person standing next to him. The guy glanced over at the nudger, saw he was looking at something over his shoulder, turned and — seeing me — pulled his lips tight while stepping back from the doorway. He sauntered into an adjoining room and started cackling.

"There's our nature boy," the director announced as I entered her office. I continued blushing as everyone politely dissipated after getting a look at their resident park nudist. Once the director discreetly inserted into the conversation that I might want to either pack an additional change of clothes until spring arrived or take a canoe with me on the trail, I did my best to change the topic. As I did so, another employee with a clipboard and a wry smile appeared beside me. He stood there and patiently waited for the two of us to finish our discussion.

"So before I, ugh, went skinny dipping, I heard another one of those Missouri tree snorers," I proudly informed the director. I had even made sure to add "on Blue" and not "on Blue Trail" to mimic the parlance of the park employees. I figured my environmental acumen and casual use of trail lingo might, however slightly, offset my occupational ineptitude.

The individual holding the clipboard broke out in radiant laugher. Startled, I turned and looked at him. Unsure what was so funny, I turned back to the director. She had her hands over her mouth and her face was turning red. When the guy dropped his clipboard in order to grip his stomach as he doubled over in pain from giggling so hard, my boss lost her composure. Hearing the commotion, all of the employees who had been gathered around her office moments before returned and looked back and forth from the man who was now kneeling on the floor and the director, who was on the verge of hyperventilating. Between desperate gasps for breath as if she were in labor, she warned everyone, "I . . . I might pee!"

After several minutes of the two of them nearly regaining self-control only to succumb to an involuntary snort, which invariably started the other giggling again, the guy with the clipboard addressed the crowd.

"Professor Freeze here said he'd heard a tree snorer out on Blue yesterday."

Everyone burst out laughing. A few even pointed at me. I politely smiled, waiting for someone to explain why my nature observation was so humorous.

After several more minutes of false stops and starts, and once everyone had slowly moseyed into the recesses of the visitor center as muted chortles seeped out from under closed doors, the director looked at me and, wiping a tear from the corner of her eye, said, "That sound you're hearing, the Missouri tree snorer I told you about . . ."

She paused. I nodded, acknowledging that I was following along.

". . . it's . . ." she snorted again and then took a deep breath, "it's just the trees rubbing together in the wind. Oh, and by the way, I need you to go out tomorrow and oil the deer because . . . ," she quickly added as her voice began to crack, ". . . *because they've apparently got a little rusty as of late.*"

With this, someone in the next room broke out in uncontrollable laugher, tore open their office door, gasped "Oh God, I gotta get some air," and ran out of the building.

I held my stupid grin and thought about this: I'd stood petrified in the middle of the forest weeks prior, believing that someone had been stalking me before convincing myself that deer squeaked. Afterward, because I hadn't bothered to research the animal which I had been told was the source of the strange noise, I'd sat in the wilderness enjoying the soothing sound of two sticks rubbing together.

I went home and, after a few online searches, discovered that Missouri tree snorers did not in fact exist and deer *snorted*, which was information that would later save my life when I once again found myself naked in the woods.

Chapter 6

Of Vultures and Splinters

As winter slowly melted into spring, I eased into my place at the park. Over the ensuing weeks, despite being only a few minutes in any given direction, I could find each and every trail in less than half an hour. Having learned the hard way as to why the rake had been abandoned in the corner of the tool shed, once I got tired of being toppled by overgrown berms, I consented to using a McLeod. My legs acclimated to the hills and I noticed that, despite the daily high beginning to rise, I was drinking less water. I attributed this to my cardiovascular system constantly improving. I quickly gained 20 pounds despite getting eight or more hours of exercise each day. This was because my Thoreau-approved, ascetic lunch of apples, cheese, grapes, and carrots was being converted into dense, sinewy muscle. My feet begun to assume the appearance of gnarled tree branches after they hardened to my boots and I started spending my weekends proudly pumicing five-days' worth of hard-won callus build-up. And, sure enough, the next time I heard the elusive Missouri tree snorer, I froze and waited. Without my jacket swishing with every step as I kicked up leaves, when the creaking resumed, I followed the eerie noise straight up. Above me, two amorous branches slid back and forth across one other, squawking with each pass.

Although I roughly knew where each of the trails resided, it took me a lot longer to learn their individual intricacies. This is the reason I was caught accidentally shitting in the middle of one. In my defense, it was my first time on Pond. When the urge struck, I went off-trail and roamed around until I found a fallen tree with a comfortable limb at just the right height which could support my weight. Being in no particular hurry, I had brought along Don Kurz's *Trees of Missouri*. It hadn't taken me long to recognize the value in being able to tell whether something was hardwood, semi-hardwood, or softwood since timber density determined how long it would take me to chop through a downed tree.

I was learning about sweetgum trees when I heard a patterned rustle of leaves in the distance. I started to frantically gather myself and my things. As I did so, Mr. Kurz sprung from my grasp and landed where he shouldn't have. My hand instinctively chased the field guide before stopping just in the nick of time. I stared down in disappointment before realizing where the book, and what it was resting in, happened to be: the middle of the trail. Mouth agape, I stood mystified while peering up and down the pathway, trying to reconcile how it had magically reappeared. I had taken so many twists and turns attempting to find the perfect spot, I hadn't noticed the footpath looped around and ran parallel to my wooden toilet. When voices became audible, I remembered the urgency of the situation and continued getting dressed. I had just finished buckling my belt when two females appeared over the nearest hill. Startled by my presence, they quit talking. I smiled at them. They smiled back and quietly continued making their way toward me. Then one, and inevitably the other, looked down and frowned with repulsion before issuing me condemning sneers. The book's unnatural shape had drawn their eye. Not knowing what else to say, I mumbled, "Pffft. Bears. Whaddya gonna do?" to which the hiker nearest me caustically replied "Teach them scatology" as she sauntered past. Unclear as to how the study of vocal bebopping related to bears, it was only after I got home and double-checked the meaning of the word that I realized I'd been made. I prayed the two girls weren't park regulars.

This was one aspect of my new job that I hadn't anticipated and it took me quite some time to grow accustomed to: meeting people on the trail. Shortly after most of the minor debris had been cleared from the forest pathways in the wake of the devastating ice storm, I met my first set of hikers. I was halfway through chopping a juvenile poplar which had unfortunately been in the fall zone of a much larger sycamore on Orange when I heard voices emanating from a nearby stand of native cane. This alarmed me and added another surreal element to being surrounded by bright, evergreen cane leaves amid an otherwise denuded deciduous forest. I had grown graciously accustomed to the serenity and near silence that the wilderness provided in the middle of winter. I stopped, propped my foot on the log and placed the ax head next to it so the handle could serve as a makeshift arm rest. I stared at the bend in the trail where the cane grove ended and would be producing people at any moment. Two adults and a small child emerged and slowly made their way toward me. As they did so, I noticed they were speaking Swedish. When they walked past, the father nodded and his wife smiled. The little, pig-tailed girl bumbled over to me and offered her hand, which I gladly shook. I watched as the family disappeared into the forest. I stood there contented. It was one thing to *know* my labors were allowing people to better enjoy the wilderness. I was now reveling in a whole other level of satisfaction after getting to *see* it for the first time.

Later that same week, as if humans were slowly coming out of hibernation, I met my second random nature lover. I was in a marsh and almost through a waterlogged maple when I heard approaching footsteps. A solitary, older gentleman waltzed along as he darted his head back and forth to either side of the trail. When he was less than 30 feet from me, I was still unsure whether he knew I was there. Just as I was about to shift my weight in order for my movement to alert him to my presence, he turned, nodded, and stopped at a conversational distance. Without a word, he reached in his back pocket, pulled out his wallet, opened it, and handed me a ten-dollar bill. I looked at it, reached out and took the money and, speechless, glanced back up at him. I was unsure his intention and humored whether he was soliciting an hour of homoerotic forest naughtiness with a lumberjack. The thought quickly followed that my presumed prostitution price tag was depressingly low. He smiled, muttered "Danke," (German for "Thank you"), and walked on down the trail. Long after he'd left, I continued to stand there, daunted. I was humbled that someone would appreciate what I was doing enough to offer me a tip, but also confused as to whether *Americans* hiked American trails.

Not all my encounters with hikers went so smoothly. Once I'd had the opportunity to put most of the maintenance tools to use, I picked my favorites and started making personal modifications to them. I wrapped a towel around the end of my ax handle and secured it with duct tape to reduce the nerve-numbing vibration. I hated lopping because after a few hours, the weight of the long-handled pruning shears begun to take their toll on my triceps. I preferred using a machete to whack through nubile branches which, if left to their own devices, would nab passersby by summer's end. Because of my tool bias, I had taken a carabiner and engineered the machete's sheath where it would dangle from the strap of my backpack. This way it was readily available and easily accessible. However, this convenience had its psychological drawbacks.

I was walking back to the trailhead late one afternoon when a twitter of incessant chatter became vaguely discernable. It had been an especially arduous day wherein a mammoth ash got the best of me after I'd lost my footing while trying to move it off the trail. The side that landed facedown had buried the broken stub of a former bough at least a foot deep, thereby anchoring the tree to the ground. As I tried to loosen its hold on the earth using a branch as a lever and another log as the fulcrum, I fell in the middle of the muddy pathway, pulling my back in the process. Having gotten my fill of nature for the day, I started heading back. As I ambled along, sweaty, caked with mud, and huffing as I went because the impact of every other step sent a surge of pain up my right side, three teenage girls crested the hill before me. At the first sight of me they froze, went dead silent and, without a word to one another, collectively turned and ran away screaming. I stopped and looked around to see what had frightened them. I saw nothing. Then it occurred to me as my machete swayed back and forth below my left elbow: *I* was what had scared them. The haggard, machete-wielding psycho killer who roams the woods that they'd seen in countless horror films had come to life. I realized that this might be a good time to ask for neon yellow, lime green, or florescent orange shirts with TRAIL MAINTENANCE — or at least NOT A CRAZED MURDERER — blazoned across the chest, lest the park's attendance begin dropping off.

Not long after I permanently scarred the psyches of a trio of teenagers, I entered Purple for the second time in my life. Purple was the pathway that my wife and I had crawled out of with our lives and little else several years before. While pacing the park during my frustrated attempt to find the tool shed, I'd deduced which trail had been the culprit and made a mental note to prolong exploring this particular section of the forest for as long as possible. However, my time had come. Although I had learned a lot that fateful day, Purple wasn't done teaching me. Like a Greek siren, it lured me in under the pretense of apology for having nearly taken my life. Once it had regained my confidences, the trail showed me what happens when you give nature the finger.

As I walked along, surveying the environment, I suddenly stopped. Despite the life-long trauma Purple had induced, I didn't recognize anything. Thinking at first that this was selective amnesia at work, I had the uncanny feeling something else was at play: We had charted the trail's length in July. It was now approaching the cusp between winter and spring. It was amazing how the wilderness changed faces throughout the year. Though seasonally overcast, since the forest's canopy was devoid of light-inhibiting leaves, the wilds were better lit and less claustrophobic. I turned back toward the trailhead. I could still make out my car. I hadn't noticed that when I'd entered, the ominous trees which guarded the trail's threshold were still there, but because they no longer labored under the weight of heavy foliage, Purple's foyer was less intimidating and now more open, more receptive. I proceeded to go up, up, up and over a series of three inclines. Since it was much, much cooler, the trilogy of rises passed by relatively unnoticed. But I knew where I was because I remembered the trail's junction. I thought back to my wife chasing after the tick I'd flicked off her. To the left was a ridge and to my right were the recesses of the forest. Since the pathway looped around, it didn't really matter which direction I chose. After a whimsical moment's thought, I turned left.

By this time in my park tenure, I had perspired the realization that unless the temperature was below 20 degrees, trail maintenance never necessitated a coat. Although still calendar winter, it was reasonably warm, 38 degrees, and I was wearing a long-sleeve shirt with the sleeves rolled up to my elbows.

As I started down the ridge, a slight wind began to pick up. Instead of gradually subsiding or increasing in strength, it steadily blew. Whereas I had been very comfortable moments before, I was alarmed at how quickly I'd become chilled by a mere persistent breeze. I shivered and unfurled my shirt sleeves. Five minutes later, I relented. I slinked off my backpack and took out and donned the windbreaker I'd tucked away in case the 30-percent chance of rain opted to rally. Once my body heat filled the inside of the jacket, I felt a little warmer, but the wind persevered. I was cold less than a minute later. Any residual body heat I managed to accumulate was immediately swept away. I kept walking, trying to think of other things in hopes of taking my mind off of the spine-pinching draft. I sped up. This did no noticeable good. I moved to a galloping sprint. This merely doubled the air friction on my face and stiffened my cheeks. I quit running.

Finally the ridge wrapped around a hill behind the prevailing gale. I stood there, safe from the arctic zephyr, and huffed into my hands while frantically rubbing them together. I stomped my feet in order to get circulation back into my lower extremities. I was shocked. I could not remember being that cold in my life. Of all the things I would come to fear in the park, the one which remains ever-present is wind chill's daunting capacity and deadly speed.

Having regained some of my body heat though I continued to shiver periodically, I started hiking again. Thanks to Kurz, I now recognized the tree whose name I couldn't recall during my first day on the SCT: It was a beech. Still tenaciously clinging to thin branches, its dry, short-stemmed, beige leaves — whose composition and texture was like water-stained rice paper — rattled frenetically in the malingering crosswinds. I passed over a dried creek bed that housed miniature ponds under an enormous awning of tree roots. My eyes followed the length of its trunk.

It appeared to be hundreds of feet tall. I was speechless at how it continued standing upright despite being only half-rooted to solid ground. From the brook, I began ambling up what slowly grew to be a massive hill. The trail had been worn by erosion to the point where the adjoining ground met me at eye-level. The hillside became terraced. Someone had installed water bars at the edge of each tier, which conveniently doubled as steps, so as to direct water off the footpath. When I reached the top, my head swooned. I could see across the Mississippi. I had previously stood on the river's banks and peered over at Kentucky, but never from 220 feet above the water. I was now facing Illinois. It was one of the most beautiful sights I had ever seen.

But my wife and I had walked this trail. At first I couldn't fathom how we had missed this life-changing panorama. Then it occurred to me: In our heat-stunned daze, we were so preoccupied with seeing the end of the trail, we hadn't taken the time to notice anything on, around, or within it. I then understood why the preceding gale was so bitterly cold. It had been coming off the Mississippi, which was busy transporting marshmallowy, premature ice floes downriver.

I stepped onto a rock ledge that projected out over Old Man River. As I flipped up the collar of my windbreaker, as if on ironic cue, the wind suddenly relented and the sun briefly broke through the clouds for the first time that day. It seemed like nature was finally, warmly welcoming me by extending an invitation to sit down and have lunch. I graciously accepted.

Once I finished eating—fearing that if I didn't do it, the task might go undone—I laid down, propped my backpack behind my head, and assumed the role of cloud supervisor. I rarely had an unobstructed view of the heavens. A perpetual blanket of stratus clouds lined the atmosphere. However, much like observing the night sky, the longer I stared at the celestial fog, the easier it was to detect the clouds' subtle nuances in consistency and color. Out of my peripheral vision, entire sections seemed to break rank by dropping and shifting to the right or the left, but as soon as I tried to focus on them, the mobile segments jumped back into place.

Lying there, optically playing with the aerial cotton balls, something very dark and very big blew by me, mere yards from my outstretched feet. It had been preceded by its fleeting shadow, which had swallowed not only me, but the *entire* rock ledge. I sat bolt upright and looked around. At first terrified, curiosity got the best of me and I stood up. I stepped forward and slowly peeked around the overhanging boughs to my left, the direction the U.F.O. had flown. A large bird soared along in the near distance. I watched as it circled several more times before diving down and out of sight. I was mesmerized because it had never once flapped its wings. It wouldn't be the last that we'd see of one another.

With lunch over, I set to work on the protruding branches that were too big for a machete. I spent the remainder of the afternoon contentedly cutting limb after limb with my folding saw, gradually making my way back to the junction. Around three o'clock and as a capstone to a very satisfying—and enchantingly mysterious—day, I brought out my pipe, a Christmas gift from my father-in-law. Alongside puffs of sweet-smelling Hamiltonian smoke, I continued sawing away as I waited for another leisurely hour to pass. Despite it being the middle of the afternoon, I was already laboring amid the wilderness twilight since the sun had started easing itself between the surrounding hillsides.

I was bisecting a limb that hung slightly above my head. The wind had returned and was entertaining itself by gusting in one direction and then another. I had a propensity for getting things caught in my eyes, so I'd long ago adopted the habit of wearing safety glasses when engaging in any activity that involved airborne debris. Nonetheless playing it safe, I immediately ceased sawing mid-branch as the breeze shifted and started blowing the sawdust toward me. Once it changed directions, I resumed my pruning. We played this game for several more strokes. When the wind died down after a rather strong surge, I quickened my pace. But it had balked. As soon as I pulled back on my saw, drawing sawdust from the cut which summarily ran down the length of the blade, a zephyr caught the pulpy particles and blew them back into my face. The current had managed to swirl the miniature wood chips up and over my earpiece and into my eye.

Being accustomed to eye injuries, I kept my eye open, retrieved from my backpack the compact I had stolen from my wife's makeup kit, and folded my trusty bandana into a neat, sawdust-extracting point. Holding my eye open wide, I glanced into the mirror, but didn't see anything. I let myself blink. I felt pressure. I searched my eye again. Nothing. I blinked a few more times. I felt a slight twinge of pain. I packed up my things and, still puffing away at my pipe, returned to the visitor center so I could inspect my wound under better light.

I walked into park headquarters and entered the bathroom. I stared into the mirror. Although my eye was extremely bloodshot and the other had begun forming a sympathetic spider web of red around it, I found nothing. Ominously, sinus congestion started setting in. I decided to go home and, as I had countless times before, let my peeper heal itself while I slept.

On my way out, the director walked around the corner and asked me how my day had been. Before I could say anything, I noticed she was scrutinizing my inflamed eyes. She then spotted my pipe, which I had taken out of my pocket as I left the building. This was not good.

From where she stood, her park nudist whose hobby was sending teenage girls screaming from the woods was now waltzing around the wilderness nonchalantly smoking pot on company time. I explained to her what had happened and showed her my tobacco pouch. After I'd finished, we stood there silently. I could see out of the corner of my good, though cloudy, eye that she was inspecting my face, attempting to discern whether I was lying. I wiped a rueful tear and sniffled. Goaded by pity, she couldn't help but chuckle at my perpetual bad luck. Attempting to convince myself the pain was fleeting and vainly distracting myself from the possibility that it wasn't, I told the director about the U.F.O.

"Turkey vulture," she said.

I quickly dismissed the absurd mental image of a big, black bird struggling to remain airborne as—with each successive flap of its wings—the weight of the Thanksgiving centerpiece which dangled from its talons threatened to drag the predator to Earth. I looked at her and, to the best of my swollen ability, tried to raise a suspect eyebrow. Noting my silence, she glanced over at me. After being met by my semi-leery expression, she stood there trying to deduce the cause of my stifled apprehension. Then it occurred to her.

"No, seriously. That's what they're called. Turkey vultures. They're all over the park."

Still dubious, I gazed into the forest and continued to make small talk.

When I got up the next morning, my eye was a softball. With my morning oatmeal in-hand, I sauntered onto the front porch. The blinding sunlight brought me to my knees. My wife drove me to an optometrist, who removed a splinter that had migrated behind—before finally lodging *into*—the back of my eyeball. He told me splinters belong in my finger, not my eye, and that the bleeding would eventually subside, but that I should go home and sleep for a few hours. I slept the entire day.

As soon as I awoke, I made a beeline to the computer. I typed "turkey vulture" into a search engine, half expecting a satirical webpage to inform me the imaginary bird snacked on tree snorers. To my surprise, they were real. With a wingspan of six feet, the massive birds eat carrion—dead animals—which they can smell from several miles away. Interestingly, when the pseudo-predators gather together to feed, the collective is appropriately referred to as a "wake." The reason I hadn't seen my vulture flap its wings is because the harbingers of death ride the thermal winds to conserve energy.

Although Purple had bested me once again, I would soon have the last laugh.

In early spring, still too early for wood pewees to flutter onto the migratory scene as snow remained hidden in the midday shadows, I was sent upstate to take a one-day class in crosscutting. By now I had deduced that crosscutting, though it often involves an angled cut, didn't necessarily pertain to which direction a person goes about slicing a tree in half. Before the training session, my exposure to maintenance tools like the four-foot, double-handled monster that hung in the tool shed was limited to those I'd seen in antique stores, whose retirement was signaled by their blades having been adorned with paintings of pastoral landscapes. By the workshop's conclusion, I wished their role was restricted to being gaudy centerpieces over rural mantels.

At an hour which farmers deem too early to start the day, the director pulled the park van into my driveway. We had a very long drive ahead of us to a place that didn't have its own zip code. But I was nonetheless optimistic. I was eager to meet other trail maintenance personnel after discovering why I had yet to bump into any of my fellow coworkers along the trail: There weren't any. When I asked about this, the director informed me that the typical tenure for those she hired to do what I did was a single day. I surmised that roaming around in the woods from sunup to sundown, risking literal life and limb alongside incessant boredom goaded by solitude, the only available distraction being the traumatization of random hikers, all for the irresistible price of minimum wage, didn't have the allure for some that it did for me.

After driving over, around, and through valleys, ponds, troughs, streams, hills, rivers, peaks, lakes, and ridges, much of which I suspected had yet to be charted by man, we arrived at a state park that presented itself as abruptly as the mountains behind it, which was inversely proportional to the speed my car sickness had premiered. I had not been prepared for my employer's approach to vehicular navigation, which was a simple case of being unable to tell the difference between a very large, multi-windowed van that could accommodate a mobile disco and a Formula One racer. Once we parked and I contemplated seeing my breakfast for the second time that day as I regained my equilibrium, the two of us toured the park's visitor center. Shortly thereafter, the director left to conduct other business.

I entered a room which had a sign that read "Xcut Workshop" taped to its door. No one was there. I sat down and waited, eager to meet other nature enthusiasts and swap wilderness adventure stories over lunch. Gradually, people started appearing. Groups of three and four slowly filtered in, talking amongst themselves. Each small huddle was wearing identical outfits. One set had donned thick, thermal, brown overalls that morning. Another cluster wore heavyweight, navy blue jackets. Although I had failed to get the wardrobe memo, I was fortunately synchronized with myself: I had on a hoodie because it had been comparatively warm the last few days.

As one person after another took seats around me, I nodded and offered a friendly "Good morning" in hopes of initiating a dialogue. Everyone I greeted politely nodded before returning to the discussion they were having with their color-coded team members. At the late hour of 8 a.m., two elderly gentlemen entered who were also wearing matching attire. The only difference between them was that one was clad in cowboy boots and brandished a very large belt buckle that read "U.S. Forest Service." Not only did his footwear strike me as an odd choice for trail maintenance, but his open advocation of the U.S.F.S. put a bad taste in my mouth.

My wife thought an appropriate get-well gift for someone who had just undergone outpatient eye surgery was a book. She had bought me a copy of Bill Bryson's *A Walk in the Woods* in order to keep my mind on my strained eyes. Bryson has few nice things to say about the U.S.F.S. and essentially deems the seemingly benign-sounding, federal organization a hired hand of the logging industry.

As I sat, alone, at my desk and tried to ward off the remnants of car sickness, I thought to myself that I had come to learn how to cut a tree in half, not level a forest. I nonetheless listened as the cowboy introduced himself and his colleague who, over the course of the day, made a mime seem chatty. Bartles and Jaymes then outlined the history, different types, safety measures, uses, and applications of crosscut saws. Four hours later, we broke for lunch.

We reconvened an hour later. I sat down at my desk, still friendless, after having spent the better part of my break trying to strike up a conversation. Instead of a friendly chat, I had had a revelation. During the 60-minute intermission, I had pried out of one overall-wearer that he'd stayed overnight in a hotel with his coworkers, drank an epic quantity of beer, and dreaded returning to the forest. Largely against his will, a navy jacket informed me he was only doing trail maintenance because he'd been laid off from construction.

Much to my regret, the wilderness was not staffed with nature lovers. From what I could gather, I was the only person in the room who *had* read Thoreau. I was the exception to, instead of being a model for, what I assumed to be the rule. As I sat slumped in my chair and stared disappointedly at the backs of my fellow trail maintenance workers, the two instructors reappeared. Taking his place in front of the classroom, after wiping his mouth with a threadbare handkerchief and thanking the Almighty for the invention of fried chicken, the cowboy announced we would now drive up the mountain and put our "book learnin'" to use.

Upon traveling up, up, and farther up the mountain, our caravan stopped at a clearing where several logs sat at odd angles. Some were flat on the ground while others leaned, propped on the stumps that had once been their foundations. As soon as I got out, a piercingly cold, very malicious wind slapped me across the face. I buried my head in my shoulders and wrapped my hoodie tight around me. We gathered in a semi-circle before the teachers, our backs to the wind, and awaited instruction.

The cowboy asked, "Alright. Who wants to get started?"

The students gave one another sidelong glances. I stepped forward.

I was eager to put a classroom lecture to practical use for once.

Fraggle Fern would have been proud. Heck, even Papa Thoreau might have given me an assuring wink had he been there. Besides, the only chance I had of staying warm was to saw something in half. I walked up to a downed tree. I looked back at the cowboy.

"Well, son, whaddya waitin' for?"

Still slightly nauseous, cold, and frustrated by the lack of moral fiber in my peers, I had no desire to humor the U.S.F.S. cheerleader.

"I need a hatchet or an ax."

The first step in crosscutting is to remove the bark from around the area where you will be sawing so the tree's skin doesn't dull the blade's fragile teeth.

"Right you are. Just so happens I have a tomahawk right here."

Since leaving the classroom, the cowboy had strapped on a holster which housed a hatchet. He quick drew and handed me the tool.

I proceeded to peel a band of bark from around the trunk at a width that would accommodate an extended blade. Continuing to follow what I had just learned, I pulled dirt out from along the base of the log and took a bark shingle and wedged it under the tree where the saw would eventually skirt the ground. It was the lesser of two evils: Soil, and especially rocks, spell death to a crosscut's teeth.

"Alright. Good job. Now, who wants to get sawin'?"

I raised my hand and walked over to where several crosscuts had been set out. Knowing we were cutting into a pine, a softwood, I chose a lance tooth saw, which has deeply grooved teeth that curl and house the cleft wood shavings with each passing stroke. By this time, a navy jacket had stepped forward and silently volunteered to help.

The key to crosscutting is to have a well-sharpened and set blade with a full set of teeth (otherwise it snags). A crosscut will do its best work if its teeth alternately extend an equidistant fraction of an inch from the tool's spine. A row of teeth which have been properly aligned makes the cutting gap, or *kerf*, slightly wider than the blade itself, but does not give it enough room to play as the saw moves back and forth. This postpones the top of the blade from getting pinched as the log gradually closes in on itself as you cut deeper into the tree.

I set the edge of the saw on top of the bare trunk and slowly pulled it back and forth to fashion a guide groove for the blade to follow. I then nodded to my fellow sawyer. Unlike a single-man saw where the operator must push and pull as well as maintain a constant downward pressure, a two-person crosscut team makes cutting through a tree very, very easy and literally reduces the work — not by half — but at least 75 percent. The weight of the tool generates enough pressure on the wood that the sawyers need only to pull and guide, guide and pull. I drew back as my crosscut buddy merely channeled the blade to make sure it didn't wobble or jar as it came toward me. Once his handle was an inch from the log, he pulled in his direction and we reversed roles. The two of us gradually found our rhythm which, in crosscutting terms, means determining your partner's pull strength, rate, and distance, i.e., force, speed, and when he or she typically stops sawing. Once established, whoever is pulling can begin tilting the blade ever so slightly toward the ground with each drag. This makes the blade catch more firmly on the corner of the cut and creates a slight rocking motion, similar to an infinity symbol. To an observer, it resembles a boat languidly undulating on a set of gently lapping waves.

When we were three-quarters of the way through the tree, the log started to pinch. I called over to the cowboy and asked for a *wedge*, which is a shim for a tree. He produced one from his back pocket and I stuck the hard plastic isosceles triangle in the top of the cut. I pounded it with the back of the hatchet, thereby widening the kerf and giving the blade more freedom to maneuver. We were told this would be necessary with most large trees unless a log rests on a ridge. When this occurs, the ground generates an upward force where the cut is being made and graciously opens the cutting gap as the trunk is being worked.

Waiting to see if I would turn and ask, the cowboy had a bottle of cooking oil ready. I dribbled the lubricant back and forth over the kerf as I had been told to do. When we started sawing again, I was amazed at how smoothly the blade migrated through the trunk, and also surprised that it was still pulling sawdust out with each drag since we'd deliberately decreased the friction between the wood and the saw's teeth.

We completed the cut and repeated the process at a distance equal to the width of a trail.

But we'd made a mistake. As the two of us finished the second cut, the remaining section broke in two. However, because we'd forgotten to saw at a slight angle instead of perpendicular to the tree, the bifurcated sides fell inward and pinned the severed segment, making it impossible to move. If we had been thinking ahead, a skewed cut would have forced the log to shift its weight in opposite directions and pushed the amputated stump out for us.

I was drenched in sweat. My body heat produced a thin curtain of steam that blurred my vision. I turned and was met by the soft, misty-gray outlines of numerous crosscut teams as they continued sawing away. I felt like I'd fallen back in time. One pairing had the perfect rhythm, which made their blade twinge with each passing stroke. This is called *singing* and indicates the saw is operating at maximum efficiency. As more partners finished their first log, they migrated over to observe and admire the super sawyers. During our classroom training, we had watched a video were a man with a chainsaw raced a professional crosscut team which, I now understood, could get their saw to sing by simply looking at it. They finished seconds after the chainsaw had completed its cut. This is undoubtedly how the B.L.M. crew had polished off so many trees in such a short amount of time.

Once the dynamic duo had finished their duet, the cowboy called us over to a tree that had been sheared at shoulder-level. The stump still supported its giant, 100-foot stalk even though it was now resting at an 86-degree angle. Because the log sat at a height which would require a crosscut team to stand on tiptoes to cut it, the tree had to be undercut or *underbucked*. The cowboy removed the bark from the bottom half of the log before grabbing an ax and slinging it parallel to the underside of the massive timber. The ax stopped dead and the middle of the handle levitated just below the strip of naked wood. Next, he took a crosscut, flipped it upside down and, resting the spine on the ax handle, set a guide groove. The cowboy then turned, looked at me, and stepped back. I walked up and started to pull. Because gravity was working against me instead of for me, I had to push up while dragging and shoving the blade across the trunk's surface. Even though the cowboy held the end of the ax handle so the weight of the saw didn't drive it out of the tree, underbucking was exhausting work. We all took turns. Eventually the wooden giant fell. It was the end of the workshop.

I stood in front of the visitor center and, after most everyone had left, I called the director and asked where she was.

"Yeah, yeah, yeah," she said, "keep your pants on." After my accident on Blue, this had become a park in-joke and stock, comedic response to any requests or questions I put to park employees. "I'll be there in a second," she added, before appearing in the driveway seconds later.

As soon as I pulled myself up into the van, the director asked what I thought of crosscutting. After we blasted off, I mustered enough energy to tell her I was enthralled, but didn't have the courage to mention the saw hanging in the tool shed was a lance tooth. Our forest was mostly hardwood and semi-hardwood, which requires a blade with a greater number of shallower teeth, such as a plain tooth or champion saw. I asked why she wanted me to take the workshop instead of getting my chainsaw certification.

"Most of the trails run alongside a wilderness preserve, so we're not allowed to use mechanized equipment unless we have special permission from HQ, like we did after the storm."

I nodded even though I wasn't sure what this meant. I could already feel my car sickness prepping for an encore. The director reached down in the floorboard and handed me a book. It was a slim volume of poems by Robinson Jeffers. I had heard of him, but hadn't read his work because he was considered a minor American poet. A bookmark protruded out of the top. I flipped to the marked page. I was met by a one-page ditty titled "Vulture." It describes a man who, as I had, watches as a vulture checks to see if he has progressed far enough in his life to be a delectable carrion feast. Unlike me, he regretfully informs the flying death shroud that his time has not yet come, but that he looks forward to the day when he becomes part of the eyes that experience what the vulture sees each day. I thought to myself that the guy wasn't playing with a full deck, yet everything made sense when I learned Jeffers was from California.

I closed the book and looked over at the director or, rather, *both* of her since reading the poem had escalated my dizziness.

"So you're saying you'd like it if I was bird food? You do know there's nicer ways of saying 'You're fired'?"

She snorted. She had expected my professional literary assessment to be a tad more refined and insightful.

"No," she snickered as we careened around a ravine. "I just thought you could appreciate what Jeffers has to say since you're now a part of it. Just read it," she instructed as she nodded at the book. When I didn't respond, she glanced over at me. From her stunned expression, my face had already turned white. I was involuntarily swaying back and forth with the vehicle. She quickly added, "Whenever you can get around to it."

I rested my very hot forehead on the very cold glass of the van window and passed out.

The following weekend my wife and I scoured neighborhood antique stores for a hardwood crosscut saw. We found one in most every shop, but they were either missing teeth or their blades had served as a metallic canvas for dusty combines in mid-harvest or weathered barns gradually succumbing to their own mortality. By the time the local vendors flipped off their lights on Sunday evening, we had long since departed for the next town in hopes of finding the Holy Crosscut. I arrived at work the following Monday with my backpack and a saw-shaped hole in my heart. For several consecutive weekends, the hunt continued as we expanded our search radius. It was April when my wife called out to me from a dank, moldy basement of a three-story, ramshackle building in the long deserted, downtown commercial district of Small Town America.

I bounded down the basement steps. As her hand rose to point toward a stationary handle, champion crosscut while asking, "Is that one any good?" I was already reaching up and over her to my newfound love.

When I brought it to the check-out counter, the shop owner was unable to reconcile why I was so giddy. I possessed neither the aura of an antique aficionado or the look of a country homemaker. I didn't even haggle over the $20 price tag. I paid and dashed out the front door.

As we'd traveled from one antique store to the next, I'd routinely checked to see if debris from the winter storm lay nearby. The proprietor and my wife watched through the storefront's plate glass window as I scurried across the road and tried out my new toy on a rotten branch. The blade was so rusty, it hung up a quarter of the way through the bough. But I didn't care. With a little love and kindness, I knew I could bring my three-and-a-half-foot, oxidized girlfriend out of retirement. She had yet to saw her last tree. I called her "Dolores."

As soon as we pulled into the driveway, Dolores and I darted out of the car and disappeared into the garage. I immediately set to work sanding her blade and, following the instructions from the crosscut video I'd watched after returning from Ice Mountain, continued playing doctor by smoothing her wood handle before treating it with boiled linseed oil. Sometime later, my wife moseyed over to where I was working.

"Do I need to start worrying?"

I had been so preoccupied, I wasn't quite sure what she'd said once I realized she was standing next to me.

"What?"

"Do I need to start worrying that you're going to leave me for that saw?"

"Dolores."

"What?"

"The saw's name is 'Dolores,'" I said as I slowly extended my arm down the length of her supple blade and admired the rigidity of her spine while my fingers gently, yet firmly, clasped her handle.

"Fine. If you've decided to leave me for . . ."

"Dolores."

" . . . Dolores, then you need to tell her to get started on dinner."

I took Dolores to work with me the next day.

With my newly acquired — and I might add hard-earned — skills, I quickly discovered that the decision to chop or saw a log largely revolves around four basic factors:

1. If a downed tree is too broad for an ax head, crosscutting is sometimes the only option unless you want to spend the remainder of your life whittling away at an oversized twig.

2. Sawing will also be necessary if a log is petrified, meaning it is completely dry and has cured. This will become apparent when a tree laughs after the ax ricochets off its surface.

3. Crosscutting is the only viable solution if a downed tree is waterlogged because chopping implements are, at best, only marginally more effective than beating the soggy timber with a dead fish. Instead of woodchips, you wind up with splintered, mushy pulp.

4. If it is the onset of spring and the poison ivy has begun to leaf out, all crosscutting should be restricted to emergency tree removal until late fall. Otherwise, an ax handle-distance from the forest's understory is highly recommended.

I learned how important the last variable is the hard, insanely itchy way.

Eager to get it on with Dolores, I was ambling along Blue because a newly fallen tree had been reported on our longest trail. However, progress was slow. Spring rains had arrived and due to the northern ice melt, portions of the pathway, along with Purple and Orange, were underwater. The regional floods gave mosquitoes and buffalo gnats, or black flies, more real estate in which to breed. Fortunately I'd inadvertently stumbled across a solution to the airborne menaces: After standard safety glasses had failed me, I'd purchased a pair of goggles. I found they conveniently served the triple purpose of protecting my eyes, keeping the gnats at bay, while also bringing a smile to hikers' faces. But there was another hurdle in getting to the downed tree: Blue and Orange had been designated by the State as equine trails. Horses are a problem for everyone on a forest trail.

Tired of playing hide-and-seek with a thunderstorm that had arrived at the park the same time I did, I took shelter in the visitor center. As I waited out the spring shower, I started thumbing through one of the many brochures lying around the building. I was only halfheartedly reading when I came across a semi-familiar name, Susan Fenimore Cooper. Unclear as to the context in which she was being mentioned, I wrote her name down and, once I got home, looked her up on the Internet. To my surprise, she was the daughter of famed American novelist James Fenimore Cooper, best known for having written *The Last of the Mohicans*. Susan had coauthored books with her father, as well as published a few of her own, and is considered one of the earliest nature writers. I checked out her most notable work, *Rural Hours*, from the local library.

One of her themes, and major concerns, is what she views as the epidemic of weeds that riddled her yard and the surrounding countryside. Her worry is not that of a landscaper or gardener and, unlike most homeowners, isn't content to merely treat the symptom by killing them, only to have the foliage grow back; she goes to the philosophical root of the problem. Her anxiety stems from having noticed that the voracious vegetation happened to be non-native varieties. Because they hadn't originated in the area and — in biological terms — *coevolved* with other regional organisms, there were no natural predators to keep their numbers in check. As a result, the alien greenery reproduced relatively unabated and subsequently choked out their indigenous cousins. American gardeners see this every year as Japanese beetles destroy rose and raspberry bushes. An ecological avalanche ensues. Using Cooper's example, as the insidious, foreign invaders suffocate endemic flora, animals that *did* evolve in the region have less to eat and, consequently, *their* numbers decline. These types of aggressive creatures are labeled *invasive species* by biologists.

Letting horses roam the woods created many difficulties for me as a trail maintenance worker. Admittedly, the modern horse evolved from a comparatively small, forest-dwelling creature. However, as a result of its having grown vastly larger and better suited to the dry, flat plains over thousands of years, even with selective breeding stemming the physiological tide, the animal meets this hilly, now-alien terrain with difficulty. And the environment doesn't fair much better.

During rainy seasons, horses dig deep cuts and grooves in the trail. All wilderness pathways have holes here and there, a.k.a. "ankle biters," which—if hikers aren't watching where they're going— can turn an ankle. Whenever the earth is saturated, everywhere a 1,000+-pound steed plants its hoof becomes an ankle biter.

To make matters worse, horseback riders also have a reputation for not respecting the trail. Because they are much higher off the ground, they can often see where a prescribed route leads before someone on foot. Due to this height advantage, they frequently take shortcuts through what are called *switchbacks*. Switchbacks are walkways which wind back and forth over the course of a hillside. Their purpose is to break monotony, ease travel, and prevent erosion. Roads that wrap around a mountain use the same engineering principle. This navigation design disperses the pull of gravity and, though more time-consuming since it is *not* the shortest distance between two points, is safer to traverse. The terraced system also curbs erosion by slowing the momentum of water and heavy-footed hiker alike.

When an equestrian takes the liberty of scooting down a slope instead of following the switchback, the horse's hooves create off-trail ankle biters in the soft, uncompacted soil. Harmless at first, the holes begin to wash due to the incline. With each passing storm, they get longer and deeper. The fissures' expansion results in their inevitable conglomeration, which further intensifies water flow. These maintenance nightmares oftentimes remain hidden under the surrounding foliage and leaf litter until they reach the trail. By then it's too late. They have transformed into full-blown erosion trenches that channel rain over a switchback the same way the vertical lines cross the "S" in a dollar sign.

As icing on the cake, when horses defecate, they spread invasive grass seed far and wide. This makes even more problems for hikers. Not only are they already limited in where they can step on a trail full of ankle biters, muddy washes, and horse poop (unlike dog walkers, I had yet to witness an equestrian clean up after a horse, which wouldn't be necessary if a manure bag was hung from the harness), they have to be on the lookout for ankle-rolling wads of equine-planted, non-native grasses. The type of feed riding horses are given produces wispy tufts of nimble foliage which are all but impervious to a yo-yo and pulling them up by the root leaves an erosion-inviting depression that, even when filled, compromises a pathway's integrity.

With my saw draped over my shoulders, I bounced from one side of the trail to the next because its center had the consistency of soupy oatmeal from horses repeatedly traipsing through the mud and a murky, manure-sheen floated on top of the puddles that had accumulated in the ankle biters. Along the way, I fought off an atomic cluster of gnats whose incessant infatuation with my facial orifices was in direct violation of several states' sodomy laws. They left me no choice but to wrap a bandana around my ears, nose, and mouth. With my goggles, I now resembled a kamikaze bandit looking to hijack a maple. All the while, I swatted mosquitoes which were plunging into my forearms like darts at regular five-second intervals. By the time I arrived at my destination, I had made the solemn oath to burn my picture of Thoreau.

The tree was massive. Its trunk stood over waist-high and had landed on top of a ridge. Its roots dangled 15 feet over the hillside to my left, and its crown hung in the air 60 feet away and 40 feet from the ground to my right. Remembering the cowboy's crosscut lecture, I thought I might be able to cheat the fallen idol. Instead of having to cut it in two places and rolling the stump off the trail, there was a good chance the tree's own weight would pull it off the ridge once I'd split it in half. As soon as I set my guide groove, I was met by a pleasant surprise. I had assumed it would be torturous to use an overgrown handsaw by myself, but Dolores did her fair share of the work even though I was obligated to push and pull the blade.

Fleeing the midday sun, the mosquitoes subsided several hours later, but the gnats decided to stick around and supervise. I was three-quarters of the way through the champion log. An individual who was either a true nature trooper, masochist, or hopelessly lost had persevered through the muck and bugs long enough to find me playing lumberjack at the back of the trail. As he made his way toward me, he stared straight ahead like a traumatized zombie while mechanically flinging his hands at his face every few seconds in the vain attempt to get a moment's reprieve from the aerial pestilence. His strident gait indicated he had no intention of stopping to chat. He did, however, do a double-take when he passed by: To reduce my backpack's weight, I had rescued an empty bottle of toilet bowl cleaner from the trash. It was much smaller than the vat that cooking oil came in and had a squirt-top dispenser.

From the hiker's perspective, some guy was out in the middle of the woods having a grand old time pouring toilet cleaner all over a dead tree. Given the circumstances, I feared this might be the individual's mental breaking point and wouldn't have been surprised if he suddenly ran off the trail and into the woods, never to be seen or heard from again.

I had cut back as much of the surrounding vegetation from around the behemoth as I could, but deliberately avoided the strangely phallic, pale white shoots about an inch in diameter, almost alien in appearance, that seemed to prefer huddling together. Most of the other young, moisture-filled spring upstarts were malleable, resilient, and resistant and refused to be snagged by the blade of my folding saw. Whereas I had begun sawing the trunk while standing upright, then crouched before kneeling, I was now sitting amid the undergrowth like someone rowing a canoe. When the tree finally started splintering, I was vertical once again, but bent over with my forearms inches from, and parallel to, the earth. I kept sawing. The mastodon began to crack and pop. I scrambled backward. The cracking and popping was joined by an eerie creaking. The noise grew progressively louder as the tree slowly surrendered to gravity.

After about 15 minutes, the log finally broke in two. The

individual sections catapulted into the sky at such a rate of speed, I instinctively jumped back. As I did so, I watched as an apple I'd sat on top of the trunk went up, over, and through the forest. I assumed I would either find it in the visitor center parking lot, pulverized by its own weight upon impact, or hear the zombified hiker yell "Ouch!" off in the distance. When the tree first fell, it landed with such force that it'd pushed the ground out from around the ridge. Now the clods of dirt which had wedged themselves into the trunk were dislodged and raining down around me. I was in the debris field of crosscut fallout. I was humbled by the power of nature.

Once the show had ended, I walked over to clear the stage. I pushed the lips of the tree's soil casing into the impact crater and smoothed out the pathway. As I did so a loud creaking— ominously similar to that of the log I'd just finished cutting had made before descending into opposing valleys—echoed down the trail. I turned around. A towering hickory started leaning listlessly before gaining momentum. I watched, my disillusionment leaving me speechless, as another colossal forest god fell across the trail.

I stood there, uncomprehending. My mind was not able to contend with what it had just witnessed, so much so that I failed to notice the gnats, which were taking full advantage of my sedentary position. I then realized a poignant irony. The first two houses I'd lived in had trees fall on them while I was inside. Either nature had heard rumor I was now listing her as my home address and staged a thematic housewarming or, out of what had long since become tradition, was still trying to kill me.

I decided it best to leave the hickory for another day. I walked over to get my saw and backpack. When I reached down, a spot of dirt on my pants shifted to the right. It seemed to have moved on its own accord. I looked more closely. A tick. Then I noticed another. And another. My pants were covered. I stood up and, pushing my chin into my chest, found they were all over the front of my shirt. I then felt something move on my neck. I started to frantically pick them off but, like a mythological hydra that spawns two heads for each one decapitated, every tick I removed led to the discovery of a handful of others. Because I had to stand very still in order to pluck the clinging bloodsuckers, whose legs functioned as eight miniature crochet hooks, the gnats rallied. People who believe they've heard Bigfoot's anguished cries in the remote, lost wilderness had simply been upwind of a trail maintenance worker futilely extracting ticks while on an equine trail whose trees were falling all around him during flood season.

A little over three hours later, I entered the visitor center. I went into the bathroom, stripped down for old times' sake, and began removing as many ticks as I could find. I glanced at myself in the mirror. It looked like I had chickenpox. They commenced at my ankles and ended at my hairline. After half an hour of alternating between mining ticks and freaking out, I got in my car and drove home.

A few days later, a rash started to break out on both forearms. At first it looked similar to the tiny bumps which had sporadically cropped up on the backs of my hands and wrists since March. Until then, I had assumed the skin irritations were insect bites. However, by the next day the rash had spread, become more inflamed, and other islands of red were beginning to appear all over my body. The day after that, the original protuberances had developed into blisters and a majority of my body looked freshly sunburned. I had poison ivy.

As I'd moved back and forth, assuming various postures and positions while sawing the massive tree, the young shoots that had limboed under my folding saw blade had been poison ivy. Not content with casual exposure, I'd beaded my forearms with a fresh line of dermatitis-causing urushiol with each passing stroke of the crosscut from the plants I *had* managed to shear as they steadily seeped juices out of their wounds. To make matters worse, I'd routinely wiped sweat from my brow with the back of my forearm. To make matters even worse, I'd used nature's restroom several times throughout the day. The finale occurred when I engaged in systematic, full-body tick removal using the same infected hands.

On the ninth day, upon returning from the doctor who had given me a very large steroid shot with a serrated, square needle to aid what he referred to as an "epic case" of poison ivy, I sat in my oatmeal bath and read the literature the director had sent home with me after I had shown up to work fully mummified: I was swathed in bandages because my blisters had ruptured and were oozing plasma.

During my recovery, I learned that from the time of contact, a person has 20 minutes to sterilize the contamination, otherwise it's too late. Rubbing alcohol is a miracle poison ivy solvent. Contrary to popular belief, once a rash forms, the damage has been done and can no longer be transmitted from one poor sap to the next. The outbreak itself is, in fact, a minor chemical burn. People mistakenly believe it's contagious because less intense areas of concentration develop after the headlining outbreaks. I memorized the mantra "Leaves of three, let them be." My wife also contributed to my devil vine education. She taught me women have an aversion to "red, bumpy men" and are not the least bit aroused by any part of the male anatomy which happens to be infected. However, this was not a problem. My infestation was so severe, the act of scratching produced orgasmic waves of delight that made me consider scheduling weekly *au naturel* pilgrimages through lush, rolling fields of poison ivy. I knew that because of my park reputation, choosing to do so probably wouldn't garner so much as a second glance from my coworkers.

When I was finally able to return to work, I proudly walked into the director's office with a box of alcohol wipes and a new addition to my wardrobe. After a little online research, I'd discovered a nifty little trick to keep ticks from going where you don't want them: Stuff your pants in your socks. However, a new problem arises because debris has an open invitation to fall into your shoes. The solution is *gaiters*, adjustable spats that go over your hiking boots like legwarmers. With gaiters in tow and my shirt tucked in, I was afforded the same protection as chest-high fishing waders which, ironically, would have been easier to get on and off. I was ready to wage war with the ticks and poison ivy. I told the supervisor I was going back out on Blue and relayed the ironic tale of the falling hickory. She told me when a tree falls in the forest, the noise I hear is the sound of job security.

Chapter 7

When It Rains, It Pours (and Pours and Pours)

"April is the cruelest month." So begins T.S. Eliot's 1922 masterpiece, a 434-line poem titled "The Waste Land." Until my employment as a trail maintenance worker, this had simply been a line on a page, albeit a line fraught with metaphorical import and potential. Now I saw it for what it was—a big fat lie—because Eliot grew up in St. Louis and no one forgets what a Missouri summer is like. If the Nobel laureate had been truthful with himself, the opening verse would start out, "June's a bitch."

When summer officially arrived, spring showers had long since worn out their welcome. The rain culminated by inundating the region with almost two feet of water in less than three weeks. The area experienced its first monsoon as the land slowly melted into liquid earth. After the ground was thoroughly saturated, water started to stand on flat surfaces everywhere. Doggedly resilient clay soil began to give way underfoot and proceeded to mildew. Finished basements that had succeeded in remaining dry for decades were now ruined. Once the sun crept through the omnipresent clouds, garden sprouts suffered dehydrating sunburn and instantly wilted because they had never experienced direct daylight.

The water table remained at ground level well into summer. As a result, a sultry humidity debuted at the break of every day. By lunch, the moderate June heat bore a heat index well over 100 degrees. There is a stark difference between dry and wet heat. Perspiration will evaporate with the former, whereas the atmosphere is already saturated in a wet heat, so convection doesn't occur. Sweat literally has no place to go other than into one's clothing. Once all available fabric is drenched, perspiration starts to follow gravity. During this oppressively muggy time, I was bringing along a fresh shirt to change into at midday *and* an extra pair of socks. The air was so heavy, it was hard to breathe and just thinking about swinging a yo-yo, plunging an ax into a log, or even *carrying* a crosscut made me thirsty. The sticky, boggy sauna therefore created a paradox. I had to lug more water around, but the increased weight in my backpack made me burn more calories and sweat even more. Water weighs almost 8 ½ pounds per gallon. I was drinking two gallons a day.

It was under these conditions that I received the news via the park director that over the weekend, the water had finally won. There had been a mudslide.

"Where?" I asked, as I swatted at the flying augers known as wood bees, which were arriving and departing from the visitor center's fascia on a second-by-second basis.

"Purple," the director replied. Like a war veteran sound asleep in the middle of a battlefield, she remained oblivious to the air traffic. She was so nonchalant about the benign bombardiers, she had her hands wedged in her pockets.

My eyes widened with joy. I almost grinned.

"Well then, I guess—" I batted at a bee that mistakenly believed my ear had been cleared for landing, "I guess then that you want me to go get a shovel."

The director stared at me. I blinked inanely back.

She leaned forward. "Mud-da sliiie-da," she said very slowly, placing extra emphasis on the final, exaggerated syllable.

Over time I'd learned the best way to counter the resident biologists' mockery was with feigned ignorance.

"So no shovel?"

Ignoring my sarcasm, the director magically produced a handful of fluorescent orange yard flags with disproportionately long wire posts. A fleet of bees instantly descended upon them. Once they realized the markers weren't flowers, they went back to aggravating me.

"Here," she said, handing me the flags. "Go set these in the corners of the mudslide. We need to see how much the ground is still moving." She turned to go back to her office before suddenly pivoting on her heels and turning about-face. "Oh, and rumor has it we have an uprooted tree on the north side of the loop. See how bad it is when you get a chance."

"Aye, aye," I said, as I offered a sloppy salute while doing my own about-face before sauntering to my car.

As I entered the trailhead, the first sizable tree to the right—a vigorous, mature birch—was leaning at a 30-degree slant. Unlike the hickory from a few weeks before, the birch apparently liked the lighting at that particular angle because it just sat there instead of surrendering to gravity. It was partially uprooted, but content to stay where it was. I had never seen anything like it. The ground was so wet, completely healthy trees were simply toppling over.

Hikers quickly learn to watch where they step due to ankle biters, sunbathing snakes, exposed tree roots, and the occasional lazy turtle waiting to play the part of a slippery banana peel. If I wanted to look at something, I came to a complete stop, inspected the landscape, and then proceeded along. Midway between the trailhead and the junction that kick-started Purple's loop, the trail suddenly ended. I looked up. An intimidating incline which peaked 20 feet in front of me had swallowed the pathway. Our naturalist would later announce a substrata of limestone underscored the bluff I was standing on. Following the ground's new hypotenuse to the right, I could see where the waterlogged soil had simply slid off the smooth bedrock. Since a section of earth had been cleft from the hillside to make a level walking surface called a *bench*, the trail abruptly dropped off into a gully. I looked down and to my left. Wet clay dangled over the cliff and a small mountain of dirt filled the creek bed far below.

I smiled. I had my retribution. Purple would have to be closed because there was nowhere to reroute the entrance. Although the

117

trail had beaten me up and taken my lunch money time and time again, I had finally won. Still, I needed to set the flags.

Before beginning my ascent, I hung my backpack on a nearby branch. I'd started making a habit of this when I left the trail because I was the master of getting lost. I had recently stepped off Orange to relieve myself and, so as not to inadvertently avail an anonymous hiker to an unexpected natural beauty, moseyed over to the next hillside while making sure the pathway didn't mischievously follow me as it had on Pond. No more than 30 feet from Orange, after an average urination which I graciously issued a rating of 5, I realized I had lost track of where I was. It took me so long to find the trail, I had to stop and pee again amid my own search-and-rescue attempt. I began to get worried when I stumbled into a dense thicket of strange, waist-high, black-and-green banded plants. Leafless, they looked like candy-coated dinosaur tails jutting out of the ground. The director later informed me I had encountered one of the most primitive of plants, horsetails. Now, with my backpack resting at eye-level, I could make out the trail at a distance and, if Purple did get to have its final say in respect to me, hikers could at least inform my boss that the park was short one nudist.

Since the trail had been cut into the side of a bluff, there was no good entry point. The mudslide had made a sheer 70-degree clay wall in front of me. I checked to see whether I could access its peak more easily by starting farther up the trail. An insurmountable gorge cut through and around the preceding hillside. I had no choice but to try to climb straight up a mud partition comprised of large, very wet clumps of soil. Fearful I might lose my footing and fall off into the ravine, I tethered myself to a stalky, extremely secure, well-rooted elm. The last thing I needed was to be face up in nature's ditch with an uprooted tree lying on top of me for good, Mike-ending measure. I had begun carrying rope so I could lasso and pull down broken, dangling tree crowns which hung ominously over the trail. I'd also found that it came in handy when I was underbucking because I could bind both the ax head and handle to the bottom of a log.

As soon as I stepped into the mud wall, my right boot disappeared. I instinctively jumped back toward the trail and reassuringly solid ground, but my foot decided to stay behind. I came down hard on my ass. Knowing better than to leverage myself with my other foot because I could lose it to Jabba the Hill, I leaned over and grabbed a sizeable rock. I placed it between the mudslide and the sole of my free boot. Pushing with my left leg as I clasp my right thigh and pulled with all my might, the slimy brown muck made a repulsive slurping sound. My enslaved tootsie slowly, gradually started edging toward me. Then the sludge monster let go. My knee instantaneously met my mouth.

Like a prizefighter who lands one last blow while receiving the knockout punch, Purple had literally placed one dead center.

I rolled over on my side, writhing in pain. I could taste blood. Haggard and breathing heavily, I brought myself to one knee and slowly stood up. Like Rocky Balboa after he'd made it to the top of the Philadelphia Museum of Art's iconic stairway, I thrust my arms in the air and screamed, "Damn you, Purple!" I wouldn't have been surprised if everyone in the visitor center stopped what they were doing and turned to look out the window, believing they'd just heard the forest curse itself.

I'd had enough. Even though the trail had sucker-punched me after the bell had sounded, I was determined to make it up the mudslide and set my markers. I willfully plunged my right foot into the wall of mud in hopes that it would stop once it hit something solid. Surprisingly, it did. I could feel a feral root or entombed branch below my arch. I pushed myself up and repeated the process. My left boot met nothing but squishy mud. I shimmied it back and forth, thinking I might rub up against another rootstock or a rock that I could use as a pivot, but there was nothing. I looked around. A sapling, buried halfway in the dirt, jutted out of the vertical tar pit two feet above my head. I grabbed hold and tested its grip upon the earth by incrementally adding more weight. Content it was a safe anchoring point, I committed. In accordance with Murphy's Law, just as my head started eking past my handhold, the miniature tree began to shift.

119

I had no choice. The sapling would eventually give, but if I was quick about it, I might be able to draw my knee far enough up I could thrust my foot into the hillside at approximately chest-level. I went for broke. A few heart-pounding moments later, I realized I was still adhered to the mud wall and not staring up at the sky from the bottom of the ravine. With another series of sweaty-palmed steps, the mudslide's plateau came into distant reach. Fortunately, a juvenile poplar sat on the edge. I reached gingerly around, took my folding saw from my back pocket and, after carefully unfolding the blade, slung it at the tree. Its teeth sank into the poplar's trunk. I pulled myself up and over. My entire front was sheathed in a thin, murky veil of mud.

I untethered myself and stood majestically, arms akimbo, glowing atop my first summit. Once I'd scanned the landscape, my head swooned as my hands darted around to the seat of my pants. My left hand was met by the Audubon Society's *Field Guide to Insects & Spiders*, a sarcastic gift from my wife after I'd come home covered in ticks. I'd crammed it in my pocket before I set off on the trail. My right pocket was empty as my folding saw rested on the ground next to my feet. Knowing better, I felt my front pockets. Nothing. My eyes shot over to my backpack down below. Jumbled against my water bottle in its mesh sleeve, the flags dangled tauntingly at me. Dejected, I collapsed where I was.

As I sat there, the wet mud gradually giving under my body weight as water rose to the surface and seeped through my pants, I noticed something move in front of me. A bug. I got out my guide. It was a wingless, therefore female, red-and-black velvet ant called a cow killer, which is in fact a type of ground wasp with a powerful sting. She had paused before a hole in the unstable terrain and, finding nothing of interest, was on her way again. Equally surprised that I had spotted the insect *and* found a match in my field guide, I looked around, squinting, on the off chance other critters might present themselves.

A scarab beetle bumbled through the mud clots which, proportionally, were the size of boulders. It disappeared under a decaying leaf. Just as the tip of its shell slid from view, a centipede emerged on the opposite side of the wilted foliage. The leaf acted like Clark Kent's telephone booth and magically transformed one bug into another. Although the sanctity of the centipede's home had been violated, a small snail, its periscope eyes fully extended, continued unabated along the leaf's curled periphery, taking no notice that its world was rising and falling amid the commotion. No more than six inches away, a bristly caterpillar was making comparatively better time. I sat admiring its single-minded focus and relentless determination. During its travels, the wormy larva disrupted the strident food-gathering efforts of something torn from the pages of H.G. Wells' *The War of the Worlds*: a harvestman—what I, as a child, referred to as a daddy longlegs. A rancid insect dangled below the scavenger's cephalothoracic pod of a body, which was suspended on eight elegant, wiry, towering limbs. The rotten carcass bounced up and down, occasionally banging against the earth, as the spider ambled along.

The wilderness was very much alive. It was only after the forest forced me to sit and take notice that I stopped to appreciate the fact. Even though catastrophe had struck, every creature had immediately begun reconstruction as their individual contributions slowly rebuilt an organic city.

It was quiet despite it being early morning at the commencement of summer. As soon as I realized this, a faint but fervent chirping broke out. I looked up. At first all I saw was the underside of the forest's canopy, which was backlit by the emerging sun. A sudden flutter pulled my eyes over to a cluster of black silhouettes. I stood up. I couldn't make out the birds' colors, only their forms. As I turned away, I noticed a strange discoloration under a nearby beech just outside the mudslide's periphery. The foliage beneath the tree appeared charred, as if scorched by acid. I followed gravity's trajectory. A densely woven army of white, wooly aphids were nestled together on a branch several feet above my head. When I raised my hand, the bleached sheet of dryer lint comprised of hundreds of huddled insects functioned as a single, larger organism and did a perfectly synchronized, collective wave. Scores of the creatures jetted out a spray that landed on my arm. Alarmed, their liquid defense didn't seem to harm me, but I nonetheless wiped it off and looked back down at the mysterious burn next to my feet. Although I could not account for the anomaly, in exchange for my confusion, nature kindly provided me with an answer to a different question. A few yards from the aphids' home, the phallic, alien shoots I'd seen earlier in the year had donned an umbrella of green leaves. I remembered looking at their plastic facsimiles in the visitor center. They were the highly toxic mayapple.

Within a few short months of being out in the woods, my perspective had changed. Before, I looked upon the natural world in awe and mystified bewilderment. Now, no less daunted, I stood fascinated by its splendor and solemn dignity.

At the recognition of the energy all around me in the wake of a catastrophe that dwarfed my own, my deflated morale started to recover. I very carefully eased myself down the way I'd come and only slipped when I was a few feet from solid ground. I grabbed the flags and repeated the process. My ascent went much more smoothly this time, probably due to my positive mindset. Once on top again, I positioned the surrogate survey markers in the far corners of the mudslide before moving down the trail.

After noting the birch's waterlogged lean was far from trade-marked because a portion of the wilderness seemed to be sitting at a freeze-framed tilt, metallic green flies began materializing before me on the trail. I assumed they had been there all season and I'd simply failed to notice them. With stunning consistency, each one dashed off unseen into the forest's camouflage at the exact moment I leaned forward to get a better look. Turning left at the loop's junction, I came upon the rotten, hollow trunk of a still-standing tree. Placid water rested in its base, but my eye had been drawn by cascading flickers of light which radiated up the trunk's empty core. Mayflies were spawning and hundreds of tiny, ephemeral ghosts floated up and out, their translucent bodies consumed once they met the bright sunlight. It was one of the most beautiful things I had ever seen. As I turned to walk away, on the opposing side of the long-dead tree, a fist-sized wad of lime green caught my attention. It was a luna moth. Fearful I might spook it,

I eased over. Before I knew it, my face was mere inches from the massive wonder, yet it just sat there as if someone had pasted it to the petrified wood. Below its conical, pipe cleaner antennas, the top of its fore wings hosted a burnt umber ridge that looked like a manicured unibrow. But this wasn't the most interesting thing about the Lepidopterian giant. Each wing housed a curious black, white, and beige dot. Although the four spots at first resembled half-closed eyes, upon closer inspection, they transformed into puckered lips. Fascinated with my discovery, I stood entranced by the eloquence of its hind wings, their tips lolling in the air like satin curtains.

With the skittish green flies as my guide, I continued through the woods while keeping a casual eye out for any deviations in the forest's understory that might signal the presence of other captivating creatures. As I did so, I stumbled upon several tears in the trail's surface. They ran deep enough that I could see down to the next layer of earth. I stared at them, perplexed. They looked like the fissures which form when parched top soil dries and cracks in the arid, sun-baked summer heat. But the ground was soaked. It then occurred to me that I was standing over the early stages of yet another mudslide. Moisture as its lubricant, the dirt was succumbing to gravity and slowly pulling itself apart. I peered down the trail. There was the uprooted tree.

A gargantuan oak, which had been one of the forest's overlords, had fallen. The tree had loomed large on the edge of the trail for decades. When its crown finally met the earth, its *rootball*—the sum total of a plant's root system and the dirt it takes with it when its owner finally keels over—scooped out the pathway, leaving a waist-deep, 25-foot-wide asteroid crater in its wake. I stepped into the flooded cavity and ran my hand along the oak's chert-riddled toes. As I stood at the mastodon's center, its shadow veiling me from the midmorning sun, I felt an emotional ease wash over me that I realized was Father Thoreau being right once again: I nodded in recognition of the term "Mother Nature" being spot-on because I suddenly had the sensation of being oddly safe, as if I'd been transported back to my childhood home. I walked over to the trail's periphery which, due to its recent transformation, now provided me with the perfect chair. I turned and hoisted my butt up on the soil ledge, propped my arms behind me with my palms facedown on the cool, comforting ground, and peered out into the wilderness. As I kicked at the muddy water just below my feet, I thought to myself that I couldn't remember having ever been so relaxed in my entire adult life.

When I returned to the visitor center later that afternoon, I gave my report to the director. She stared at the floor and contemplated the implications. I could see the weight bearing down on her at the prospect of losing our most popular trail.

She suddenly came out of her administrative meditation and looked up at me, smiling.

"Well, we won't know until we know. Go out tomorrow and see how far the flags have moved so we can get an idea of ground movement."

I didn't like the sound of this one bit. It meant there was a chance Purple might persevere and continue to be the bane of my existence.

After giving the order, my boss hurriedly spun back around in her chair. This was deliberate. She was avoiding me.

During the last few weeks, I had adopted the hobby of picking interesting plants and bringing them back to her for identification. Her emphasis in biology had been botany. She was so good at spitting out a name as soon as I placed a flaccid stem with wilted leaves in front of her, part of my thrill came from watching her botanical acumen at work.

I cleared my throat.

She slowly turned around.

"Whaddya got for me today?" she asked.

I had five for her, two of which I thought might pose a challenge.

"Lamb's quarter, toothwort, garlic mustard," she shot out, before adding that all three happened to be coincidentally edible, which she followed with a pensive frown. "Actually," she continued, "I'd suggest eating as much of that one as you can." She was pointing at the mustard.

I looked up at her, my ever-present confusion having long since become a permanent facial feature.

"It's invasive," she informed me.

I nodded in learned acknowledgement and silent pride that I understood the technical term.

It was time for the bonus round. I'd made a point to pluck a flower which, to me, looked like a hundred other white blossoms with a yellow-button center.

"Star of Bethlehem," she declared without hesitation.

She was right. She was always right. I went home each day and double-checked online, a habit I'd gotten into after failing to do follow-up research on Missouri tree snorers had me leading a one-man snipe hunt. Yet I was about to put an end to her hitting streak. I'd selected a fern, not because I found it intriguing, but every single one looked exactly like the next.

"Maidenhair fern," she announced.

I looked up at her and then back at the fern.

"Are you sure?" I asked.

She rolled up her sleeve. On her shoulder was a black-and-gray tattoo of the fern I'd picked. I knew it was the same one because the palm fronds eloquently spelled out the plant's name. I never doubted her botanical judgment again.

"Hold on a second. Don't move," she instructed before disappearing into the recesses of the visitor center.

She returned with two books.

"Here, take this home," she said, as she handed me the first one, Edgar Denison's *Missouri Wildflowers*, "and see what you can do with it." Then she offered the next, Annie Dillard's *Pilgrim at Tinker Creek*. Its cover announced the book had won the Pulitzer Prize. I looked up at her. I wasn't aware biologists went out of their way to read Pulitzer winners' work; that had been my job.

"What?" she said. "It's a book. Read it."

I went home that evening and, once I'd researched and found that the acidic burn beneath the beech was sooty mold, a fungal byproduct of the honeydew the aphids spewed all over me, and confirmed the director had been frustratingly correct on all five botanical counts once again, I began reading *Pilgrim at Tinker Creek*.

It was obvious from the first page that Dillard has an ear for language and control over the written word. In my professional experience, a lot of nature writers are biologists first and happenstance authors second. Although such prose is informative, it rarely makes for good reading. At the end of his life, Thoreau openly questioned whether writing about the natural world could be aesthetically appealing or, in order to do so satisfactorily, had to be done with an objective, sterile pen. I'd seen the difference in my students. Science majors are trained to avoid the subjective adverb and adjective and merely report on the facts using steadfast nouns and numbers. "Pretty" has no place in science. Conversely, those focusing on the Liberal Arts are told that *how something is being said* is as important as *what is being said*. They are taught not to admire touch, taste, sight, sound, and color, but wallow in them. For these pupils, statistics are often viewed as cold, immovable, and boring *things* that arbitrarily disrupt a story's natural flow and rhythm. Nouns are the hooks upon which descriptive terms and phrases are to be hung.

A grammatological divide separates the two worldviews. Both sides appreciate exacting detail and have the shared goal of finding meaning in the particulars, but the language used to distill the world and its contents houses undecipherable dialects that inhibit communication between the two parties. Dillard does not answer Thoreau's question, but gets us closer to finding common linguistic ground. In this regard, *Pilgrim* is a bastard pidgin of sorts. I completely understood why it won the Pulitzer.

Dillard is a philosopher with a scientific eye. She gives her reader the impression that with enough time, she could extract the meaning of life from a grain of sand. The key to her success is that she does not look from the outside in. Instead, she accepts the quantum Möbius strip called the Observer Effect, which states watching something alters the behavior of the object but, more importantly, also changes the observer's perspective. The tales contained in *Pilgrim* are fluid and the author's examinations of what she sees around her fascinating. Subtle themes and motifs run throughout the text that weave together universals of nature which are easily missed. Like a scientist, Dillard acknowledges the darker side of the natural world yet, like an artist, she sees the inherent beauty in what most label horrific (even within themselves), such as the crimson roses painted by the blood-drenched paws of a housecat. She makes her audience realize that cannibalism, predation, and parasitism are not only part of the circle of life, but essential to nature's creative process. It seemed serendipitous that the director handed me this book hours after I started seeing nature for the first time. Dillard further honed my vision.

Eager to see the woods through my new Dillardian glasses, I drove straight to Purple's trailhead the next day. When I reached Mount Mudslide's peak, I thought I was in the wrong place. There were no flags. None. The plateau even seemed different in some inexplicable way. Then it occurred to me what had happened. Some hiker, probably teenagers, came along and yanked up the flags. I would have to go get more and start my geological survey afresh. But before I did so, I moseyed over to the edge of the soggy avalanche with the intention of projecting a glorious, multistory stream of urine into the gully below, which — if things went as planned — would automatically merit an 8 out of 10 due to novelty. As I neared the muddy rim, I noticed an oddly shaped, slightly bent, streamlined twig protruding out of the dirt where I'd placed one of the markers. I crouched down for a closer look. It was a flag post. I spun around and glared at the three other corners. I found no others. The ground was moving at such an unstable rate, it had swallowed every single flag overnight.

I smiled.

If the malevolent trail had consumed the flags just to make my life difficult, it'd finally overplayed its hand. I now had a legitimate reason to close Purple forever.

I climbed down, did my best impression of Julie Andrews as I skipped back to the trailhead, hopped in my car, nearly broke the land speed record on the way to the visitor center, and delivered the "bad news."

"Well," the director sighed, "I guess we don't have a choice. Go on back and start putting branches and whatever else you can find across the trail to keep people from going in."

I was ecstatic. I had the exclusive honor of slamming the door on the trail that had literally bruised, battered, and bloodied me. I dashed back to Purple.

I spent the remainder of the day amid yawning fields of poison ivy and pillaged for branches and logs to set in the pathway. The technical term for what I was creating is *scree*. Although, in theory, seemingly easy work since I was standing in the middle of a forest, broken boughs weren't in coincidental abundance right where I needed them. In some areas, I had to traverse a handful of hills and stumble into neighboring valleys to find the necessary supplies and then carry or drag them back to the trail.

During my lunch break, as I sat on a waterlogged stump, something moved next to my thigh. I looked down. As I scrutinized the rotten log, a small lizard rose out of its lichen-encrusted bark. Careful not to frighten it, the thumb-sized reptile cocked its head and begun studying me when I scrunched my nose in an attempt to stave off a sneeze. It then scurried onto my leg. With the delicacy of a surgeon, I slowly lowered my upturned, outstretched hand. To my surprise, as soon as my knuckles met the top of my thigh, the prehistoric creature darted into the center of my palm. After a few seconds, the heat from my hand lulled the little guy into a soporific trance and it closed its eyes.

While I sat there playing adopted father to a sleeping baby dinosaur, I thought back to my recent nature epiphanies on the trail. I then turned to look at the work I'd completed. The sudden movement startled my miniature friend and the lizard jetted off my hand and landed unseen in the foliage below. The director would later tell me that I had been thermal host to a fence lizard and, noting they are typically coy and timid, called me "Lizard Whisperer," a titular mock-up of a television program about a professional dog trainer who has a way with canines. Taking its abrupt departure as a sign, I began gathering more wood.

Once I'd finished, the first 100 yards of Purple was impassable. Amid the strangely soothing, atonal soundtrack of cicadas' mating drone, I draped caution tape between two trees that guarded the trailhead. Despite the revelations I'd had in that portion of the park, I wished good riddance to the cursed trail.

The entrance was not impassable. It was now *very* passable.

When I arrived the next day, the director informed me that I needed to check on my "old friend." I could tell by her tone that she was referring to my park nemesis, Purple. I got in my car and headed into the forest.

I slammed on the brakes as soon as I saw what she had been talking about. The caution tape — now tapes, *plural* — waved in the wind from their respective trees. As I approached the pathway, I could see that all of the branches and logs I'd laid across the trail were gone. However, this is not what infuriated me most.

In the unlikely event that a hiker might mistake my scree for lackadaisical trail upkeep, when two trees stood adjacent to one another along the wilderness corridor, I'd built a wattle fence by stacking and interweaving limbs into a wall of wood. I wanted to make sure that when I got done, only the blind would have doubts whether Purple was closed for business.

The first wattle wall I'd constructed, just inside the trailhead, had been destroyed. There was little doubt in my mind that the others I'd painstakingly pieced together farther down the walkway had met the same fate.

Although I first humored the possibility that Purple had sent its woodland fairies to do its evil bidding during the night, I knew that devoted fans had simply refused to let go of their favorite trail. I decided that even though someone had laid waste to my previous day's efforts, covering the path once more — this time all the way back to the junction — might permanently discourage any adamant trekkers. It took all day. When I was finished, and as a preventative capstone, instead of a single strand, I wallpapered the trailhead with caution tape.

At the end of the following week, as I drove toward the visitor center, I noticed the director was standing outside speaking to someone. When I started to pull into the driveway, her chin dropped to her chest, a Kubrickian grin crept across her face, and she jutted an extended thumb in Purple's direction.

The shithead had done it again. Whoever was responsible hadn't bothered removing my sheet of caution tape, but simply walked around it, because the undergrowth to the right of my giant DO NOT ENTER banner was trampled. Once more, my scree was gone. It was time to take evasive, hiker-inhibiting action. I gathered all the thigh-sized logs I could find and sheared them of any limbs. At staggered, half-foot intervals, I placed the smooth, lathed lumber end-to-end on, and parallel to, the trail. When I was through, it looked like an army of oversized rolling pins were streaming down a dirt river. If anyone tried to step on Purple, the person's shoe would catch and roll on the large, unstable branches. After a few paces, the culprit would hopefully retreat to another unobstructed, more ankle-friendly footpath. I took wrist-thick limbs and drove them into the center of the walkway for good measure. With one less trail to worry about, I set about my work in the park.

Approximately a week later, I entered the director's office and, exhausted, threw myself into a chair. It had been a long day and I was looking forward to having the next two off. She swiveled around to face me.

"Bad news."

She didn't have to say anymore. I was irate.

"Why?" I protested. "Why do people go where they know they're not supposed to unless, you know, they need to . . . ?"

"Technically, they can go wherever they want in the park."

At first taken aback by her declaration, I took the initiative to verbalize what I assumed was the understood insinuation.

"Just not off-trail."

"No. Sure they can," the director affirmed. "We can't stop them. It's their right. All *we* can do is try to discourage them."

I paused and thought about this. Most likely a consequence of my postmodern indoctrination, I had presumed the trails were the human boundaries of the forest. I was treating the earthen walkways as implied guardrails which cordoned off the natural museum. For me, they served the same purpose as the velvet ropes in bank lobbies that silently ushered patrons to cashier desks. In reality, the trails were more a friendly suggestion than a barked command.

The director sat looking at me. My face betrayed that I was hopelessly searching for new ideas.

"Just put another stretch of caution tape out in front," she said. "I'm having the sign removed next week."

I drove down to Purple. The bandit had stripped away my wallpapered warning, yanked up the stakes, and kicked aside most of my ankle twisters. I futilely taped off the start of the trail once again. I stood at the trailhead thinking about people's place in nature, half hoping a vehicle would pull into the parking lot that had incriminatory license plates which read "SHTHED" so I could give the perpetrator a piece of my mind. Unfortunately, no one drove up. Then my mental light bulb flickered on: It was Friday. The director had told me about Purple's previous violation exactly a week ago and, on the first occasion, seven days before that. This meant the vandal was entering the trail on Thursday, most likely in the late afternoon or early evening.

I watched and waited. The caution tape remained intact for the first half of the week. Thursday after lunch, I kept myself busy — and more importantly on the park's interior roads — running errands for the director. Regardless of where a particular task resided, I made sure to swing by Purple on the way. Having checked the flood levels in the lower campground, I was driving back to the visitor center when I noticed a truck parked at the trailhead. It was almost five o'clock.

I sped up. As the nose of my car dove into the gravel parking lot, a guy reached out and tore the caution tape in two. Although I was exasperated, I made a point to memorize his sadly non-descript license plate number, 370H55V, so I could report it to the park ranger.

"Hey," I yelled as I slammed my car door, while almost adding "Shithead" at the end. By this time, he had entered the trail and was bending down to grab one of the logs left over from his last scree-clearing excursion. "Why'd you do that?" I asked, point blank, as I marched over to him.

Slightly startled, the trail outlaw turned around.

"What?"

"Why'd you tear down that warning tape just now?"

"Cuz it's not supposed to be there."

The lunacy of his response begged the question. I thought that if I established myself as a park authority, he might relent.

"I work for the park. We put that up to keep people from hiking the trail. There's been a mudslide."

He paused before rebutting, "I can go anywhere I want. This is a state park, ain't it?"

Apparently he'd conferred with the director while plotting his trail decimation campaign.

I was speechless. All I could surmise was that I was standing in the presence of a trail liberator, a freedom fighter willing to die for the cause as he railed against the tyranny of state park employees who sit in their offices devising new and interesting ways to oppress the hiking masses.

My blood was pumping because there was no logical explanation for his actions. But I wasn't willing to let things slide.

"We blocked this off because it's way too dangerous to hike now. Trust me. You could slip and fall and die in there."

He thought about this for a second. Just when it seemed that he was on the verge of consenting, the shithead said, "Yeah, but I got the right to die out here if I want."

I could hope for — but not argue with — that.

Soon after we'd closed Purple, I learned that hikers — like water — follow the path of least resistance unless, of course, they're shitheads. Taking a break from yo-yoing an overgrown SCT, I was having lunch in the visitor center one afternoon when the

133

director walked up to me mid-granola bar.

"We got one down on Pond. Rumor has it the rootball is right off the trail."

I tossed my snack in my backpack and took off. Whenever a tree falls across a trail, if it sits more than two feet off the ground and its base is less than a couple of yards from the pathway, a new route will be worn around the log in a matter of days. Though seemingly harmless, these hiker-made thoroughfares — *social trails* as they're called — deviate from a trail's engineered design and, like horseback riders' shortcuts, can become erosion free-for-alls. I feared it was already too late.

It was already too late. The damage had already been done. A smooth, clear walkway led around the tree's foundation and on up the trail. I set to work and in a little over an hour, the obstacle was no more.

A few days later, I was lopping along Pond when I arrived at the area where I'd removed the tree. The foliage on the social trail had not begun to recover and the rogue footpath had, in fact, gotten wider. I quit what I was doing and, as I had on Purple, piled up as many trekker-blocking branches as possible. I then went about my way.

I came back the next day to finish pruning the other side of the trail. My scree was gone. The shithead who'd eradicated my labor of love on Purple had apparently caught wind of my recent efforts and expanded his territory accordingly. However much I wanted to believe this, I knew it was highly unlikely. As I stood there, staring at the infuriating damage, an idea came to me. Perhaps the reason people were tempted to remove my obstructions was due to their blatancy. I thought back to Fraggle Fern merely tossing leaves over the trail once he'd finished planting the baby cedar. With Purple, people knew a trail existed, so there was no hiding the fact, but because this one deviated from the established pattern, hikers wouldn't expect a detour unless they saw the reroute or knew it was there. Although midsummer, I set about finding a variety of decomposing leaves, small twigs, and even dug up a small shrub and placed everything on the illicit walkway. I made it look as innocuous as possible. Then I heard someone coming.

At first I prepared myself in case the hiker wanted to stop and chat. Then it occurred to me to run and hide so I could see firsthand how effective my trail decoy was. I crept up an adjoining hillside as quietly as I could before melding into the lush, heart-shaped leaves of a squat catalpa. A chipper, slightly graying retiree with his thumbs wedged in the straps of his backpack came moseying down the pathway. Nary a care in the world, he looked merrily to his right and left as he plodded along. He arrived at the reconstructed area and, without a moment's hesitation, stayed true to the original route. Eager to get feedback on my work, I quickly descended the hill to ask the guy if he'd even noticed a discrepancy in the trail.

It was probably a mixture of the sudden noise, the sight of someone coming out of nowhere in the middle of the woods, and — again — my machete swinging under my arm that caused the man to stumble back in fear, trip, and fall down the opposing hillside.

Before becoming part of the forest floor, he maniacally flailed both arms clockwise as if doing a vertical backstroke while he tried to regain his balance. But he lost the equilibrium battle. His backward momentum became so great, his legs slid out from under him and *he* was the one who was suddenly turning clockwise again and again as he rolled head-over-heels down the hill. In the process, one of his shoes came loose, flew up and over him, and landed with a ker-*plunk* in the pond for which the trail had been named.

After a fugue of apologies that reiterated how sorry I was, I fished the man's sneaker out of the water and escorted him back up the hill. As I dusted woodland debris from the front of his shirt, I looked up at him.

"So, uh, I gotta ask. Back there on the trail, did you notice anything different?"

Still attempting to reorient himself and figure out what just happened, the man glanced over my shoulder in the direction I'd casually nodded and then back at me, confused.

"Right there," I said as I turned and pointed. "Right where that little shrub is." I faced him. "When you came up the trail, did you think about walking where that shrub is or did you just, you know, go on down the trail?"

I politely smiled as I awaited the verdict.

He continued staring at me, looked back at the trail, then walked away. I could hear water squishing with every other step.

Chalking up my trail concealment project as a victory, I sat down and, to my surprise, found a half-eaten granola bar in the bottom of my backpack—an unexpected reward from the gods for my ingenuity.

The days were gradually getting shorter as summer wore on. Having missed it countless times before, I'd discovered a small pond not far from one of Orange's more isolated stretches. Whenever I worked the trail, I made sure to time out my lunch so that I was in proximity of the secluded basin. I enjoyed leaning against my favorite tree in the forest, a roughleaf dogwood, and watching diving beetles paddle languidly along while other bugs defied the water's tension and darted back and forth over the pond's surface like it was a sheet of tempered glass. If I was lucky, a snake would shimmy off the embankment and lead a procession of ripples as it made its way across my own private Walden. I prayed I might finally catch a glimpse of a venomous wriggler, such as a cottonmouth or copperhead, which are common to the region. My passion to spot a nasty of nature had recently been enflamed after I'd stumbled upon a dusty copy of John Mehrtens' *Living Snakes of the World* in the back of a used bookstore.

It was a good day. I had a Pulaski and was literally dragging my feet in search of exposed tree roots that might trip up hikers. A little before noon, my leg snagged on the wild roses which courageously lived right off the footpath and signaled the pond's veiled entrance. I propped my grubbing tool against the opposing side of the dogwood and, as I took off my backpack, noticed a pinky-thin yet forearm-long northern rough green snake attempting to sample my chemical trail from a nearby stump. Its tongue, which was alarmingly red in contrast to the vibrant green, yellow, and white pull of taffy that housed it, flicked in and out while I retrieved my water bottle and sat down. Throughout lunch we stared at each other and, as if we were on the same schedule, when I started to pack up to leave, it slinked off into the forest.

Being trained in literature, when I met the trail again only to be greeted by a prairie kingsnake that had managed to swallow half a garter snake as the prey hung on for dear life to its predator's tail, I should have taken it for the omen it was. The forest was in the process of consuming itself whole that day and I happened to be standing in the middle of it.

I chopped roots for another couple of hours. I decided to change gears when I came upon an adolescent pecan that had fallen between two of its siblings. The sister trees had caught their brother which, upon impact before coming to a dead halt at chest-level and perfectly parallel to the ground, had been expertly shorn in half. Where the horizontal log rested, atop the fact that it was small enough I could remove it with my folding saw, lulled me into a false sense of reassurance that nature would continue to be kind that day. As I set to work, I noticed movement out of the corner of my eye. By the time I turned my head, a swarm of paper wasps had already begun to descend. The saw's vibration had set them off.

I dropped the blade and started running down the trail. Like nagging wives on the wing, they kept in hot pursuit. When sharp, very acute stings begun keeping time on my chest and back, I stopped and tore off my shirt. I'd subconsciously thought the self-propelled, flaming hot needle-nose pliers needed a bigger target because not every wasp in the nest had filled its daily sting quota. By removing, thereby untucking, my shirt, I had also done the airborne demons another courtesy. I'd opened a gap at my waistline, wherein Team Pain collectively yelled "Carpe diem!" before diving in. Having done so, I could rest assured I would be receiving full sting coverage. Because I was wearing my gaiters, my britches were tucked into my socks. The bugs filtered into my pants and had nowhere to go and nothing better to do but sting when the mood was right. I had no choice . . .

In retrospect, going native was an impulsive mistake. I somehow remembered not to slap a stinging insect, but to swat it aside so as to keep from pushing an otherwise benign toxic plunger into me, while also recalling the fact that cold-blooded animals' metabolism—and therefore speed—increases with air temperature. The high for the day was slated to be a crisp 95 degrees, which meant they were probably able to break Mach 1. Critters the size of my pinky became impossible to evict because my hands were trembling with anticipatory fear. As soon as I pinpointed and brushed aside a handful of miniature drill bits, I started running again, only to freeze once I felt another begin tattooing me. This allowed the stragglers to catch up while giving everyone a chance to rest their wings for a second. Thankful for my gratitude, the aerial architects of anguish repaid me in kind with a new round of nipple-protruding butt poison. When the first in the latest series of stings debuted, like a Pavlovian dog, I immediately responded with "Wha." With each successive pop of the tail, the volume and duration of my rejoinder increased. It incrementally progressed from the commonplace "Wha-ha," to a more committed "Wha-ha-ha," before "Wha-ha-ha-ha" prefaced me barreling down the trail at a dead run, screaming as I went because—lest the hive miss so much as a single square inch of tender pink flesh—the inside of my mouth was the only part of my body that remained unperforated.

When I realized I hadn't been stung for several seconds, I paused and started darting my hands all over my body. After my session of self-love confirmed my persecutors had either tired of me or stopped off at the nearest venom station to refuel, I looked frantically around. My body pulsating, I knew I needed to try and lower my heart rate since I'd absorbed enough toxins to make a rhino woozy. I was standing in a corridor of brambles. *Brambles* are collections of intertwining vines and thorn bushes that typically support one another as they grow up toward the sunlight. Because they had been shorn throughout the years, they formed dominating walls of impenetrable green. I was enclosed for 25 yards in either direction. That was when I heard it. My heart rate soared.

A snort. Like a bull. Again. Pretty sure that wild buffalo had never roamed the park, I knew it could only be one thing. A deer. It was approaching late summer and what I was hearing was the warning signal of a mother doe. I turned toward the sound. No more than 15 feet in front of me stood 150 pounds of protective maternal apprehension. Clearly this was not the cute, vestal fawn I had met last winter unless she'd spent her life savings on steroid stock options. She snorted once more: a full-bodied, robust, bold nasal grunt from deep within the snout of a very, very long nose, which meant she was one of the matriarchs of the forest. Either I had come up on her so quickly that I'd startled the criminally mislabeled "gentle giant," or she was passing wry criticism on my manhood. Regardless, this was a bad sign. Because the flight response of the poster animal for fleeing had been scratched off the either/or checklist, it left only one option: She was ready to fight. My life flashed before my eyes as my mind raced forward to my funeral dedication where my gravestone epitaph read "Mauled by a deer." I had no doubt my wife would have the engraver chisel in "while naked" in parenthesis. Since I was positive the doe had made her choice, it was my turn to pick from the F or F menu. I knew that if I decided to run, I wouldn't be able to outpace my antagonist. I was equally sure the outcome would be the same if I met her head-on. So it came down to the warrior's dilemma of whether I wanted hoof-shaped indentations in my back or chest.

I chose to die a hero's death. I charged forward.

To my surprise, she leapt up and over the bramble hedge and forever out of sight. I'd forgotten deer were Olympic hurdlers.

I stopped. I was once again flabbergasted by nature. I should have been dead after hosting a wasp drum circle or from internal injuries as a result of being steamrolled by Bambi. But I was alive. As I stood there thinking perhaps I'd been selected as nature's play toy much like a mouse that's batted around by a cat for sheer sadistic pleasure, I realized that I needed medical attention, badly. I was several miles into the woods. I shook out and put on my clothes, slung my tools inside my backpack, and started down the trail.

As I hiked along, my mind in a non-functioning stupor, I could hear the faint sound of traffic far, far off in the remote distance. I remembered a portion of Orange ran alongside a highway. Down the highway was the visitor center. Knowing now that I was free to roam anywhere in the woods I wanted, I decided that given the current circumstances, it would be prudent to take a shortcut. I made a hard right and followed the noise.

In my desperation, I had forgotten about my park map, which was sleeping soundly in my backpack. It plotted the trails throughout the park, but was also topographical, meaning it charted the surrounding elevations and could have told me where hills and valleys were. Such information is useful to someone who is in a bit of a hurry because he is racing toward the eternal light.

Guided by the sound of passing vehicles, I mounted one hill only to find an impassable ravine waiting for me on the other side. This happened over and over. I'd turn around and stumble back down the dead-end hillside before impulsively going left or right. All the while, the hum of civilization would fade and then get stronger, fade and get stronger. After an indeterminate amount of time, the roar of traffic had continued to get progressively louder. I drug myself up another aspiring mountain. And then another. As I crested the peak, there it was: two-lane blacktop.

I bolted to the bottom of the hill. When I reached the road, I peered up and down the highway. Nothing looked familiar. Trees lined the pavement in both directions or, rather, someone had taken a brush, dipped it in hot asphalt, and bisected the forest in a single stroke. I paused, trying to get a bearing on where the visitor center was in relation to the trail. I knew if I made the wrong choice, the last thing I might see were the letters and numbers "370H55V" as their overjoyed owner fought to keep his jalopy in line with my head after I'd collapsed onto the roadway due to dehydration, fatigue, and gullibility. As the scene played out in my mind, it occurred to me that the shithead's license plates had been spot-on after all.

I went left. Heat waves were radiating off the searing pavement, somehow managing to make me hotter than I already was. My sweat-drenched shirt clung to each sting and, like a wood rasp, dragged the course fabric over my raw, protruding, countless wounds every time I took a step. I peeled off my shirt and tucked it in my back pocket. I quickly discovered that roadways are as frustrating as hills. Hope could be waiting on the other side, but it probably wasn't because Despair had run its ass out of town after beating it over the head with the Stick of Naiveté. Hill was met with hill was met with hill. I unscrewed the cap of my water bottle. When I raised it to my mouth, I was surprised by how light it was, only to realize it, like me, happened to be bone dry. I tried to think back to when I'd taken the final sip. My evaporated mind couldn't remember.

I had no other choice. I slunk off my backpack, sat down on top of it, and stuck out my thumb. This would be a testament to the nature of man. Despite the events of the day, I nonetheless felt hopeful because it was getting close to rush hour. If a random stranger picked me up, I knew the human race might stand a chance at persevering; if turkey vultures were fighting over Mike jerky by nightfall, I . . . I . . . I lost my train of thought. My brain had had it. It was waving the white flag. So I surrendered and just sat there, mindlessly waiting.

Perched by the roadside, baking in the late afternoon sun, I rolled the cuffs of my pants up to my knees in the vain attempt to stave off heat stroke. I noticed my shins had broken out in purple hives. The director later informed me that when I went off-trail, I entered a field of stinging nettle. The plant's infamy is so renowned, many a famed pen has given line space to the noxious weed. Hans Christian Andersen, Aesop, the Brothers Grimm, Bacon, Kipling, Pepys, and the Bard himself make reference to the perennial, whose hundreds of prickly spines act as hypodermic needles. These botanical syringes inject a toxic concoction of neurotransmitters, histamines, inflammatory mediators, and formic acid when touched. Some strains can grow to be seven feet tall, but the run-of-the-mill, two-foot variety I had inadvertently slogged through still housed thorns that could penetrate heavy-knit pants. On top of it all, I was having a severe allergic reaction to the nettle's poison.

As I stared at my poor legs, a car flew by. I turned and optimistically waited for its taillights to open their red eyes while the automobile gradually came to a stop. It fled over the next hill. One vehicle after another, and another. I thought to myself that perhaps the drivers couldn't see me even though I had made sure to camp out between hills. To make myself more visible as well as raise my spirits, telling myself that I was about to be rescued at any minute, I stood up and put on my backpack. Another car came barreling down the highway. I tried to make eye contact with the driver in hopes of evoking guilt. When he spotted me, the motorist's eyes widened and he sped up. Shortly after he whizzed by, I heard another car coming. I could make out long, blonde hair and what looked like a professional outfit. As soon as the business woman caught sight of me, she jerked the steering wheel and swerved to the other side of the road.

Dejected, my chin sank into my chest and, as if nature had finally grown tired of me and suddenly let go of the puppet strings, my shoulders involuntarily followed suit. As I stood there, absentmindedly glaring at a bleached-out soda can on the ground, I noticed my arm was strangely dry. I'd quit sweating. It wasn't that I was no longer hot; I was burning up. I'd quit sweating because all available bodily fluids had left my body. But this wasn't the worst part. I yanked my forearm up to my nose. I couldn't believe my eyes. In place of glistening perspiration, I was paradoxically covered with *chill bumps*. Either I was hallucinating as my mind tried to convince itself that it was back in the ice-covered forest of half a year prior or my regulatory system was backfiring. Regardless, something was very, very wrong.

This was when I accepted that the *Book of Me* would more than likely be the *Book of Mike* because someone else would have to tell my tale. Yet I took comfort in the fact that at least the last few chapters would be somewhat interesting. I only wished the *BoM* could have been a tad longer. Maybe I'd get lucky and a longwinded biographer would turn my novella-length life into a novel. I thought to myself that the text could be bulked up a bit if the publisher suckered some environmental group into penning an introduction. Despite her crippling sorrow, my wife might even pull herself together just long enough to suggest my portrait of Thoreau be tossed in as a tribute to her late husband's epic credulity.

Amid my lamentations of a soon-to-be lost legacy, I happened to glance at my chest. Only then did it occur to me that I looked like a sunburned elephant man with Smurf legs who had an 18-inch blade strapped to his side. Having recognized these hitchhiking-hindering variables, I knew the next sensible step was to unfurl my pants, put my shirt back on, and tuck my machete in my backpack. But I was done. I resigned myself to Fate and didn't care how my life would end. For no explicable reason I started walking down the road, the toes of my hiking boots raking the ground with each step, my heels dragging along behind them.

I do not remember passing out. I was told I made it back to the visitor center, only not through the door: I collapsed in the parking lot. I do not remember being in the hospital, where I was supposedly informed that my illogical goose bumps were the late stages of heat exhaustion dangerously bordering on heat stroke. The first thing I remember after heading down the highway once the blonde nearly drove her car into the ditch in an attempt to put as much distance as possible between her and a deformed, purple-legged, serial killing hitchhiker is blobs of color and numbers. As I regained consciousness, my eyes begun to adjust to the light. Hazy red, green, yellow, blue, and white squares floated above my head. The Tibetan prayer flags. I was home in bed. I then remembered the wasps. I felt my chest. Raised bumps. It hadn't been a bad dream; it had actually happened.

I lifted my head off the pillow and looked across the room. Blurry, black, protracted numbers began materializing inches from my face. My brow furrowed as I squinted my eyes into focus. On my chest, next to each sting, was an inverted number:

$$34, 12, 9, 28$$

My wife had either grown tired of losing count and decided to make calculation easier on herself or had done so for my benefit after the wasps made good on their promise to give me a thorough going over. When I sat up, thereby pulling my body out from underneath the covers, the numbers grew progressively larger. I tossed back the bed sheet. For the sake of variety, she had also used red ink, which I now noticed was reserved for random written and pictorial commentary. A frowning face next to the word "ewwww" rested beside a bull's-eye, at the center of which was a sting. "Ouch!" was neighbors with "Ka-pow!" and "Oooo, that's a big one!" A large X marked out my right nipple and "Nope, that's not one, Sorry" scribbled beneath it. I jerked back in terror when I spotted the upside-down cartoon wasp she'd doodled on my knee. I saw *237* on my lower left shin, which was where my wife had stopped playing Connect the Dots with a constellation of whelps that started at my hip. Having gotten a fair approximation of what the grand total might be and lightheaded at the thought of what had transpired, I fell back in bed.

I turned over on my side and despite my grogginess, realized something was sitting on the nightstand. It was a get-well card. On its cover was a kitten hanging from a branch by one paw. Someone had drawn a handlebar mustache on the feline. I reached over and propped it open so I could read the inscription. The sender had scratched out the company-produced "Hang in there" and written below it, "I told you to keep your pants on." It wasn't signed because it didn't need to be.

Chapter 8

Paradise Regained

It was probably a mixture of Dillard's conscious inspiration as Thoreau subconsciously pushed me along, atop my stubborn determination to succeed where so many trail maintenance workers had failed, that had me back at work once the summer heat finally gave in. But, after getting lost again, I knew that despite all of the wilderness knowledge I had accrued, I understood little and was still very much ill-prepared for what the forest doled out on a daily basis. I had to do something because the local hospital was considering issuing me my own parking space and, admittedly, as a Darwin Award nominee strongly favored to win top prize, it was iffy whether I'd live long enough to see the trees change color.

I had heard a wilderness survival class was being offered in late summer as a non-credit adult education course. At its core, wilderness survival is a study in anthropology. It is a hands-on look at how primitive man lived and survived in the wild. By signing up, I would learn how to build a shelter from nothing but what the woods provided, locate and sterilize water, make a fire by rubbing two sticks together, and navigate the forest without so much as a map or compass. I'd even be able to identify the plants I could eat and those that could kill me. The best part was that I wouldn't have to leave work early, or at all—the class was being held at the park.

After the first day, I was hooked. My teacher was a lanky, long-haired man with a goatee. Alarmingly handsome even by heterosexual standards, barring the tribal tattoos which ran down both arms, he looked more like Jesus than Encino Man. His glistening blue eyes bore a patient weariness as he dictated the laws of the primitive jungle with equal parts contagious energy and professional, paced reserve. I got the impression he was going to let us learn the hard way, but that we were nonetheless in good hands because his juxtaposed character implied he remembered all-too-well what it was like to be lost in the woods without a clue. To my surprise, I left the first class with a homework assignment.

I was so ecstatic about the course that when I arrived home and my wife asked how my first caveman class had gone, I simply smiled and uttered a polite "Ugh!" The students had been shown how to erect a lean-to and we had a week to build one by ourselves. As soon as I pulled into the driveway after work, I made a beeline for my shelter and continued where I'd left off the day before. My wife was not enthused that half a wooden tent with a roof made of dead leaves and tree bark was taking up space in the front yard. (However, once I added a fire pit and heat-refracting retaining wall, her lawn chair took up quiet residency next to my hut.) In the ensuing weeks, she came home to find plastic bags floating like deflated Christmas ornaments from the boughs of our prize silver maple. I checked each evening to see how much water the bags had accumulated due to the leaves' constant evaporation. She complained about the "Fred Flintstone hole" I'd dug beside the porch as my solar still dripped a steady stream of condensation into a waiting cup. The tables had turned; I had out-hippied my patchouli-scented wife. The squawking made by the friction between my spindle and bearing block woke her up one night as I doggedly tried to get a fire going in our living room. The next day, when she opened the front door to announce that supper was ready, only to find me with a greenbrier leaf I'd picked out of our neighbor's yew bush dangling from my lips, she went back inside without saying a word. Despite the Stone Age lunacy which surrounded her every waking minute, she bought me my second copy of Tom Brown's *Field Guide to Wilderness Survival* for my birthday. Its predecessor had died a watery death after falling into a puddle as I tried to figure out how to turn pond scum into something drinkable.

By the end of the course, I knew I'd never get lost in the woods again. After learning that the traditional navigation method of cutting blazes in trees and bending branches is strangely frowned upon within the confines of a state park, I started erecting *cairns*—

piles of either sticks or stones—to mark my path whenever I opted to go off-trail. I deliberately wandered into the wilderness so I could draw maps using a cartography method called *dead reckoning*. I would triangulate my position, guess how far I had traveled and for how long, and then see whether my calculations were correct by conferring with my watch and park map. Although I'd purchased a compass, I was now able to build a *shadow stick*, which quickly reveals east and west, but more often than not I let the Earth's axis remind me where I was: Since I was in the Northern Hemisphere, the sun is dominant in the south. This is why herbalists place their seedlings in a south-facing window. Barring rare environmental exceptions, heliophobic moss retreats to the north side of tree trunks and the trees' sun-loving crowns, unless they are compensating due to past or present competition, favor the opposite direction. I no longer logged on to see when sundown would be before leaving for work and then wasted energy checking the time throughout the day. Each hand-width between the bottom of the sun and the horizon gave me roughly one hour of daylight.

Following the survival instructor's rule of "Only if hunting or being hunted," I quit running through the woods because I risked turning an ankle. I stepped on top of—instead of over—fallen trees since I had no desire to startle a timber rattler that might be dozing in the log's shade. By keeping my feet perpendicular to the slope of an incline, I rarely fell down hills any longer. I ceased to panic when I couldn't remember how much of the trail remained after a long day. I knew that by arbitrarily speeding up, I was pointlessly burning energy, surrendering awareness of my surroundings, and stressing myself out.

I'd gotten my money's worth. Shortly after the class ended, a storm suddenly broke out while I was on Blue. I threw together the skeleton of a lean-to and—using the trash bag I now carried with me at all times as a waterproof roof—waited out the rain. It could also be used as a blanket, poncho, or for rain catchment. Before ducking inside my impromptu shelter, I'd placed an empty bottle at the base of my water-repellant roof. Once the sky cleared, an overflowing container of fresh rainwater awaited me.

Seventeen pounds of water weight was replaced by a three-ounce bottle of purification tablets and I skipped down the trail knowing I could find the life-giving fluid with extreme ease.

My pack weight was further reduced because I no longer needed to be a walking grocery store. I nibbled on violets, chufa tubers, plantains, and chickweed throughout the day. Once fall began to take hold, I would forage fresh black walnuts, red and white acorns, and hickory and pine nuts. I'd winnowed so much of my daily cargo that I celebrated my newfound self-sufficiency by tossing a camera in my backpack. Since they had been the catalyst for my nature epiphany on Purple, bugs were quickly becoming my passion and I started compiling a photographic catalog of the various creepy-crawlies I came across in the wild. I would also be able to document my first encounter with a venomous snake if I ever managed to spot one.

Although I hoped they would never be needed, should I ever break an ankle at dusk, I'd been given the skills to survive in the woods overnight. I could make a splint, tap water vines, locate and identify edible insects, and create a signal fire.

More important than the ability to build an emergency shelter during a freak storm, find water, or stave off hunger if I forgot my lunch on the kitchen counter was the understanding of man's place in nature. The class had provided me with a window into the past. As I vainly tried to generate my first glowing ember using a bow drill, I looked around at my classmates. Thoreau had been right. Hiding beneath my peers' synthetic clothes were the skeletons of our ancestors. In the very woods in which I stood, the Osage Indians' forbearers perfected many of the same techniques I was trying hard to—not learn—but remember. Though we struggled as our spindles cartwheeled across the ground after escaping the clutches of our taut bow strings, it became clear to me that humans were still better suited to live in the wild, where we'd coevolved as a species for 97 percent of our existence, than amid a steel and concrete cityscape, which is such a comparatively recent development that we haven't had time to properly adapt. I could see that the artificial environments filled with people whom we cannot easily recognize as part of our tribe creates unnecessary psychological and emotional stresses. The course had made me comfortable in what I now—not *believed*—but *knew* to be my natural home.

After realigning my perspective of nature and gaining a better appreciation of the wilderness and my place within it, my time in the woods became more consistently rewarding and less frequently life-threatening. However, every once in a while Mother Nature sat me down and we flipped through our family album, lest I forget my humble beginnings with her.

Erosion was getting the upper hand on Blue's trailhead. I was often met by hikers' elongated footprints, the product of people having slid down the sloped entrance, layers of which had been shorn away by perpetual traffic and late summer rains. Having noticed this but always making a mental note to come back to it once more pressing issues were addressed, the trail made a point to remind me I was just another trekker amongst many.

I'd recently had a custom sheath crafted for my crosscut in order to keep its jagged, shark-like teeth from snagging on feral foliage, or decapitating me should I slip and fall. I tested the efficiency of my new blade guard by slipping and falling down Blue's oil-slick welcome mat one morning. I stood up and assessed a situation I could no longer ignore. Looking as if I'd dove headfirst into home plate, I walked back to my car, put the saw in the backseat, and pulled a Pulaski out of the trunk. It was time to build some steps, but I didn't follow a step-by-step trail maintenance manual. I used a philosophy book as my blueprint.

Once I'd finished Dillard, I started seeking out more books about nature, especially those with a philosophical bent. I quickly stumbled across *A Sand County Almanac* by Aldo Leopold. Leopold is no Thoreau, but he doesn't try to be. His writing is much more carefree and playful because he revels in nature whereas H.D.T. marvels at it. Still, *Almanac* does what all good books do: It gets the reader's mental gears churning.

Leopold discusses what he calls the *land ethic*, which is the principle of respecting nature, not as a resource, but as an entity unto itself. Further research in this area introduced me to the concepts behind these diverse worldviews: *Anthropocentrism*, which means "human-centered," and *biocentrism*, which means "life-centered." The dividing line between the two "-centrisms" is exemplified in how Aldo and I approached the great outdoors: Leopold doesn't have issues with mosquitoes, gnats, poison ivy, wasps, or deer because from where he stands, they don't just hang around to make people's lives a living hell. He accepts that they serve other purposes, both seen and unseen. Given the opportunity, he'd have politely whispered in my ear that Satan's green trident isn't just itchy, it produces oxygen, filters toxins, helps prevent erosion, and provides food and shelter for wildlife. Likewise, I welcomed wasps into my garden once I realized they avidly hunt cabbage moth larvae to feed their young. It's all a matter of perspective. As the Southwest nature writer Edward Abbey pointed out, "From the point of view of a tapeworm, man was created by God to serve the appetite of the tapeworm." I knew this to be fact. After I'd played host to a tick buffet, I suspected the arachnids had thanked their vampiric god for providing them with such an easy, credulous meal because what other purpose could I possibly serve? Surely not my own. With this I understood the forest was neither friendly nor antagonistic. It merely *was* and it was entirely up to me how I chose to view my surroundings.

Over the course of my self-directed studies, I learned that most nature lovers adhere to the notion of a "life-centered" existence, but argue whether *conservation* or *preservation* is the best avenue by which to achieve biocentrism's ends. The terms' underlying philosophies are found in their definitions.

Preservationists strive to keep the wilderness as pristine as possible so people can experience it in its primitive state, what the director liked to refer to as "Nature in the Raw." This is why

I wasn't permitted to use mechanized equipment on the trails that bordered the wilderness area: Synthetic human noise is a preservation no-no. A seemingly little thing, a roaring chainsaw can upset migration patterns and, like a boisterous neighbor, drive animals from den and mating sites. Obviously only the devout would want to go traipsing around in the woods without a pathway to guide them but, should they so desire, the park provided the wooly, untamed opportunity. By contrast, conservationists hope to include everyone in the grand scheme of nature things, but keep a close eye on how a resource is being used. This is the main purpose of a trail: to enable one and all to enjoy the forest while not having to worry about coming across a lion exodus, tiger lair, or lecherous bears.

The difference in the two viewpoints can be seen in how the dueling factions would treat a snickerdoodle. A conservationist will ration out how much of the cookie can be eaten per day so that everyone can enjoy its buttery goodness over an extended period of time. The preservationist will put it under glass. There are obvious pros and cons to both sides. The preservationist would argue that regardless how many pieces an individual divides the baked delicacy or the amount of time between servings, the tasty delight will eventually be gone. The conservationist counters by saying that at least everyone had a chance to enjoy the cinnamon explosion because if it's relegated to being an exhibit in a pastry museum, the snickerdoodle might last forever, but all a person can do is look at it. *A Sand County Almanac* permitted me to see behind the administrative veil of the park. It became apparent that I worked alongside both conservationists and preservationists.

When the daily highs drop from the tolerable 80s into the pleasurable 70s, and the nightly lows begin steadily declining, thus signaling the undeniable onset of fall, three great migrations take place at the park: birds, people trying to get their nature fix before it gets too cold, and the conservation versus preservation debate of how to deal with the second. When I entered the visitor center one morning, I mentioned that I desperately needed to lop Orange but a large tree was down on SCT. This was a concern for me because Orange had become our most popular hiking attraction since we'd closed Purple. It was also the trail first-time park attendees were gravitating toward. Our naturalist shrugged off my anxiety.

"Let 'em get a little nature on them," he jovially protested.

But I saw it a different way. A park's funding is based, in part, on the number of people who visit each year. I knew our regulars would step over a log or push past an enterprising raspberry vine without giving either a second thought. My concern was first impressions. If a couple decides they might like to go hiking for the first time and their experience is fraught with overgrown pathways, exposed tree roots, and eye-gouging limbs—any number of which could be the tipping point—they might not ever return unless, of course, they pick up a copy of Thoreau later on down the road. To be fair, I had grown to dislike having to yo-yo beautiful hedges of purple-and-green trillium that dangled playfully over the trail, but understood, in a very Marxist manner, I needed to sacrifice day-brightening black-eyed Susans for the greater good of the park's revenue and, therefore, the park and its visitors. Besides, if I didn't urge people in a particular direction, it would be a preservationist nightmare: The masses would go willy-nilly throughout our 3,000-odd acres, ultimately killing a lot more wildlife than I did. The naturalist and I weren't arguing whether I should remove a mammoth tree which had fallen across a trail or even that Orange should eventually be pruned. We were bickering over the particulars which, in essence, made it clear I was a conservationist while he was a preservationist.

Our naturalist might have been content to let hikers get quite a bit of Blue on them until the number of complaints could no longer be ignored, but I viewed the slip-and-slide as an opportunity to sharpen my teeth on Leopold's land ethic. Using my Pulaski and starting at the top, I cut lateral, tiered trenches down the hillside while being mindful of the *outslope*. I wanted drainage, not erosion. I then rounded up several stumps that had been sitting around since the ice storm and placed them in the troughs I'd just finished digging. I now had a stairwell. Because the entrance was a bench, I'd been obligated to shear off some of the adjoining ridge to make room for a few of the steps. I gathered chert and built a dike over — or *cribbed* — the unstable portions of the dirt ledge. Four hours later, I stepped back to see what I had before me. To my surprise, I'd created a natural staircase which was not only aesthetically appealing, but also functional.

I stood and admired my handiwork. In *Shop Class as Soulcraft*, Crawford observes that one of the casualties of 21st-century, white-collar America is the loss of pride in one's work. This is because the product of a person's postmodern labors goes largely unseen. As a professor, I had been unable to observe the end result of my pedagogical efforts. Any discernable influence I might have had on my students was barely noticeable after being diluted by countless other instructors' classes, and I rarely saw how the lives of my scholastic apprentices turned out once they got their degrees and disappeared into society. Looking at my stairwell, I was witness to the impact I'd had upon the world and how, through my own sweat, I had improved it. And every time I entered the trail, I would be visually reminded of this fact. As Crawford notes:

> The satisfactions of manifesting oneself concretely in the world through manual competence have been known to make a man quiet and easy. They seem to relieve him of the felt need to offer chattering interpretations of himself to vindicate his worth. He can simply point: the building stands, the car now runs, the lights are on. Boasting is what a boy does, because he has no real effect in the world. But the tradesman must reckon with the infallible judgment of reality, where one's failures or shortcomings cannot be interpreted away. His well-founded pride is far from the gratuitous "self-esteem" that educators would impart to students, as though by magic.

It was at that moment I no longer felt like a glorified, out-of-place yard boy picking up sticks and raking leaves in an oversized, overgrown lawn. I was a bona fide trail maintenance worker responsible for an entire forest. To top it off, I'd nabbed a picture

153

of a prehistoric bug so strangely alien it's the stuff upon which children's nightmares and bad science fiction movies are made: the jumping bristletail.

I grabbed my backpack and headed down the trail. I was off to the nearest creek bed for a celebratory lunch. As I meandered along, basking in the pride of a job well done, a very loud noise broke out in front of me. I leapt back and almost lost my footing in the process. Once I regained my balance, I looked up. A towering shadow of Black Death ascended before my very eyes. And then, as suddenly as the cacophonous sound had emerged, the darkened, blurry form was gone. By the time I repositioned my heart from the pit of my throat to where it belonged, I'd pieced together what had happened.

A turkey vulture had been feasting on a dead carcass right off the trail. Because its head was buried in its food, the scavenger didn't hear me coming. Since I'd been watching where I was walking and meditating upon Leopold and Crawford's philosophies, I hadn't noticed the bird even though it stood waist-high. I chuckled to myself. The American poet Charles Bukowski once said, "We" — meaning people — "are here to laugh at the odds and live our lives so well that Death will tremble to take us." Despite being oblivious to the fact that its cold, bony hand was so close, it could have tapped me on the shoulder, my life-affirming, post-stairwell glow shone so brightly, it'd sent the Grim Reaper packing.

It was late afternoon in early fall. I'd finished the workday, but wasn't ready to leave the technicolored forest. With one of the many box elders that lined the front of the visitor center as my backrest and a patch of wild garlic for a cushion, I waited out the sun by combing through a post-apocalyptic novel my wilderness survival teacher had recommended, George Stewart's *Earth Abides*, and mindlessly picked at the seemingly endless number of frustratingly adhesive, washing machine-resistant, triangular seed pods stuck to my pants.

"Tick trefoil," a voice proclaimed behind me.

It was the director. She was leaving for the day.

"You scared the ever-loving shit outta me," I declared as I looked up at her, only to be met by a mischievous grin.

"Tick trefoil," she repeated, as she nodded at my seed-lined britches. "Glad I caught you," she went on to add. "We gotta big one down on Pond. But there's good news. One of your friends called wanting to know if he could come out and do some volunteer work for us. I said, 'Sure. Why not?'"

I thought for a second. I had friends that I knew came to the park on occasion, but they weren't likely to blur the line between recreation and work. I proceeded down my mental list, dismissing one friend after another. None came to mind.

"Two questions," I announced. "One, how big we talking?"

"Big," the director replied, widening her eyes for emphasis. "By the way the guy who'd just come off the trail was talking, I'm gonna guess at least two-and-a-half, three foot thick. Said he had to climb over it. That's all I know."

"Okay. Two, what friend?"

She nonchalantly shrugged her shoulders.

"Not sure. Didn't give his name or, if he did, I don't remember. Just said he knew you and asked if you'd be working tomorrow. I told him you were."

She stood there looking at me as I stared at the grass, trying to figure out who the anonymous caller might have been. Realizing I was preoccupied with solving the mystery and wasn't going to say anything else, the director blithely said "Good things" and walked to her car.

I'd kept in contact with a handful of former students after leaving the university, one of which had entered the professional world of business a few years before I resigned. He had established himself as a brown-noser early in the semester. His attempts at teacher manipulation were so bold-faced, obvious, and unapologetic even his classmates laughed at them. Although I had little respect for someone so shameless, his poor machinations grew to have an innocent charm. Unable at first to reconcile how a person could have so little self-respect, I slowly recognized that he knew his exploitations had a beneficial side-effect: By volunteering at every turn, he set a pro-active example for those around him and his clumsy PR often buoyed the spirits of all involved. As with most executives in training, he was always eager to please.

That night the phone rang. It was my former student. When I saw his name on the caller ID, I assumed he wanted me to look over a cover letter or was applying for a business loan and needed a reference.

After dispensing with formalities, his purpose in calling remained vague. Finally, he asked if I was enjoying my new career. I told him about my latest wilderness mishap and he laughed.

"It can't be that bad," he assured me. "Girl Scouts go hiking all the time."

I chuckled and told him that he should try it sometime.

"I just might," he said. "How's tomorrow sound?"

I paused. He seemed serious. I tried to envision him in something other than a tie. When I didn't immediately respond, he continued.

"I called today and your boss said you'd be working tomorrow. Thought I might swing by and say 'Hi.' Get some exercise. Commune with nature or whatever."

"That was you?" I said, dumbfounded. "She said someone called wanting to volunteer — "

"Yep. It was me. What all do I need to bring?"

Realizing he *was* serious, I told him that water and whatever trail food he thought he might want to nibble on along the way were both good ideas before suggesting he come to my house so we could carpool, to which he replied, "Right. Save gas. Good idea." Then, in the overly enthusiastic voice of a sales rep, he stated he looked forward to the outing, a change of pace, new experiences, and the opportunity to do a little charity work. When he mentioned the latter, I nodded to myself. The question of motive was solved.

He pulled into my driveway 20 minutes early. As I closed the front door behind me, I turned to find someone who had long since grown accustomed to slacks: His jeans fought him every step of the way. They were fashionably rumpled at the cuffs and vainly trying to hide a new pair of steel-toe work boots. I extended my hand as he approached and was met by a practiced, polished, toothy smile, which was interrupted when my student stuck a beefy cigar in its center in order to meet my salutation. I'd somehow forgotten he was taller than me and, even though it was the apex feature of his face, failed to recall his trademark boxer's chin.

"Got what you need?" I asked as he, like a veteran politician, clasped my hand in both of his. I was barely able to suppress a grin at what I anticipated would be a fairly entertaining day at his expense.

"Yep," he cheerfully replied. Eager for my nod of approval, he pulled a small bottle of water from his back pocket as something crinkled when he patted his thigh.

I nodded in approval. He smiled. We started walking toward my car.

"Beautiful morning," he said as he feigned admiration of the emerging day, a look he'd undoubtedly lifted from movies and television. "Wonderful day for a hike," he added.

With a sidelong glance, I asked "You ever been hiking?" and tossed in a raised, suspect eyebrow to keep him from embellishing his wilderness résumé.

"Nope. I just think this is the type of day that'd be good for hiking," he said, proud that he'd made an astute observation since I hadn't contradicted him.

We got in my car and after being updated on the latest stock market trends, told which tax loopholes had been maliciously closed over the past few months, and given a synopsis of his newest business model, we arrived at Pond's trailhead.

As my student watched while I pushed the ax handle through the crosscut's handhold for easier, single-handed, over-the-shoulder transport, I asked him if he was ready to go hiking.

"Yep," he reported with an overeager air of confidence.

I unclipped the machete from my backpack and offered it to him. He looked down at it and then up at me. Lines of apprehension riddled his forehead because he wasn't sure why he needed a weapon where we were going. He refused to commit by accepting it until I explained myself.

"Here," I insisted, pushing it toward him. "Whack a few weeds as we go along."

Relieved, his face lit up. He yanked the cutting tool out of its sheath and admired the abused, worn blade.

"Oh yeah," he said as he ran his thumb over countless notches and chinks. "Nice!"

After locating an overlong walking stick for myself, we headed off into the woods.

As soon as the first piece of foliage came within blade's reach, my student started frantically swinging the machete like he was defending his virtue from a trove of drunken, handsy woodland elves. "I feel like I'm in *Predator*," he said as he decapitated a flower. In less than half an hour, the rate of botanical genocide dropped considerably. I looked back. Ten years my junior, his solid build was veiled by the physical effects of living a climate-controlled, fast food-sponsored, executive lifestyle. Crescent moons of perspiration crept out from under each arm, flanked by an inverted sweat triangle at his neckline.

Noticing I'd peered in his direction, he proclaimed "Whew, quite a workout" before taking a few cursory swings at a poison ivy vine that was creeping up a tree. It folded forward under the weight of his blade and fell on him. He mindlessly tossed it aside and wiped his forehead with the back of his hand.

"Whaddya think so far?" I asked as we kept walking.

"Not as bad as I thought it was gonna be and *definitely* not as bad as you had me thinking it was," he replied. "Kinda nice really," he added while stopping to gaze off into the distance. Once the minimal period for meditative reflection had lapsed, the sound of the blade whisking the air returned.

When we came across a fairly large log on the edge of the trail, I paused.

"You wanna take a quick break?" I asked as I turned back toward him.

To my surprise, he was several yards behind me.

With my hand at the side of my mouth, I yelled, "Hey, you wanna stop a second?" and took a seat.

A grumble of "God yes" echoed through the forest before a clearer, crisper, "Yeah, sure" came bounding up the pathway.

"Hey, back that way a bit," he said, pointing with the machete as he plopped down next to me with an emphatic grunt of relief, "there's a tree growing sideways. Is that some kind of funky virus or something that does that, or is that just how those kinds of trees grow?"

"Yeah," I said, as I motioned in front of us. "It's called 'fallen down tree blight.'"

He looked where I'd indicated. A gangly persimmon sapling was folded over under the weight of a collapsed, long-dead sycamore. The tree had adjusted to its new living conditions and its lopsided branches were unanimously reaching toward the sky.

"Huh," he muttered. "How about that? Looks like a giant comb."

I glanced over at him.

"You, uh, got a little something there," I said, nodding at his chest. Several ticks were making their steady ascent up the front of his shirt.

Alarmed and slightly surprised he'd done anything that might have gotten him dirty, he dropped his chin.

"Holy shit!" he screamed. He jolted up from the log and started jumping up and down. "Get it off! Get it off!" he yelled as he thrust his hands in the air to distance himself from his affliction. To the casual observer, it looked like he was being mugged by the Invisible Man.

"Hold still," I said, as I removed one tick and then another. "You might want to tuck your shirt in and stuff your pants in your socks," I advised.

He looked at me, not realizing the implication of what I was suggesting.

"Can't," he informed me as he hoisted up one pant leg, "ankle socks." He didn't offer a reason why he wasn't able to shove the bottom of his shirt in his pants.

"How you liking those new boots?" I asked.

"Oh, these?" he rhetorically questioned while continuing to hold up his pant leg as he tilted the heel in the air and drove the toe into the ground. "They're good, a little stiff, but it doesn't matter. I plan on cleaning them up and taking them back," he said with a wink. "Speaking of, do you know if I can claim this as a tax write-off since it's charity or whatever?"

I just looked at him. Having rid him of ticks, we sat back down.

As he leaned forward, anxiously searching for stimulation, he absentmindedly took one sip after another from his only bottle of water. It was almost half empty. He pulled his phone out of his pocket and started tinkering with it.

Temptation got the better of me.

"You know, ticks know where you are because of your carbon dioxide bubble," I told him. "The longer you sit there, the easier it is for them to find you."

He bolted up and stared, wide-eyed, at where he'd been sitting.

"No worries," he reassured me. "I'll just keep moving then," he said as he begun pacing back and forth. "You know what I like about being out here?" he goaded in the best weathered woodsmen voice he could muster. "No one can get me," he said as he held up his phone, showing me he had no reception, before putting it in his pocket and using the opportunity to steal a quick glance at his shirt.

Then a sudden rustling caught our attention. I stood up.

"What's that?" he asked, at first alarmed, before offering, "Oh, there's probably other people out here, isn't there?"

I didn't say anything. The sound had instantly died away. I knew it wasn't hikers because the parking lot had been empty when we arrived. I waited for the crinkling to return or movement to catch my eye. A few seconds later, the crumpling started again and a sheaf of leaves waved at us from the adjoining hillside.

"Look," I said, pointing, "an armadillo."

Squinting, he said, "Oh, I see it. Huh. I've never seen a live one before." He chuckled to himself. "Me and my frat brothers used to pull off when we spotted one on the side of the road. We'd flip it over and put a beer bottle in its paws. You know, make it look like it was drunk off its ass."

Although I felt slightly ashamed, I also laughed at the mental image of an upturned, humpbacked armadillo, petrified by rigor mortis, nursing a cold one. I glanced over at my student.

"You know they carry leprosy, right?"

"Leprosy . . . ? *Leprosy* leprosy? Like arms-fall-off leprosy?"

"Uh huh."

"Huh. Nope," he replied as he unwittingly wiped his hands on his pants, "didn't know that. What's he doing, looking for bugs and stuff?"

"And grubs and worms."

We watched the armored scavenger sift through the leaf litter. Then my student turned to me and asked whether the trail continued in a straight line.

"It makes a loop," I told him.

"Care if I take the lead then? I kinda like this hiking thing."

"Way to show initiative," I said, mocking his business lingo.

He smiled and winked.

"You mind?"

"Be my guest."

A few steps into the trail, I watched as he wiped his face over and over. Not five yards further along, he started mumbling under his breath while he ran his fingers through his hair and pawed the back of his ears. I slowed my pace, anticipating what would come next.

"Goddammit," he yelled in protest as he turned back toward me, "all these spider webs."

"Spined orb weavers," I said as I approached. "They're all over the place this time of year," I added while jutting the tip of my walking stick at one suspended between two trees a few feet in front of us.

He turned and, once he realized what I was showing him, screamed.

"Oh goddammit! Look at those things," he said as he leaned forward, pointing, after stepping back a safe distance.

He continued to point at the spider, but then unconsciously curled his finger into his palm and, pulling his arm into his chest, wrapped his fist in his other hand to protect it from the docile arachnid. He stared with open-mouthed fascination at the dimpled and spiked abdomen that hung before him.

"They're like little rhinoceroses," he observed.

Then it occurred to him: He'd walked through numerous webs. He started swiping his hands across his chest, arms, and the front of his pants. Once he was satisfied that no eight-legged, baby rhinos had hitched a ride, I handed him my walking stick.

"Thanks, but I don't need it," he said. "I'm fine."

"Hold it out in front of you to snag the webs," I instructed.

He looked at the walking stick and then up at me as he calculated the physics of what I was saying.

"Oh, I get it," he said as he nonetheless waved off what I was offering. "Thanks, but I can get my own."

He looked around. The first thing that caught his eye was a devil's walking stick, a plant whose name is poignantly appropriate because a pole wrapped in barbed wire would be less abrasive. Enthralled by his self-sufficiency, he stepped forward and grabbed it. I cringed. I thought to myself that the only way this scenario could be any worse is if he'd walked up and hugged a honey locust. The official tree of Dante's *Inferno*, the hardwood is considered sacred by sadomasochists everywhere due to its clusters of 4-inch-long thorns.

Though he bled quite profusely, my student's reaction and the size of his wound were grossly disproportionate. Anyone in auditory range would have assumed the woodland elves had caught up to him and were busy rewriting sodomy laws. After applying pressure to his stigmatized palm and my sudden onset tinnitus begun to subside, I volunteered my walking stick once more.

As we proceeded along, my student kept the staff at arm's length in the direction the trail led while leaning back to hack at a patch of jewelweed at its periphery.

"You don't need to keep holding it out in front of you if you're not moving," I told him. "It's not a force field. They're not going to jump out at you."

"Never know," he said as he glanced over his shoulder between swings.

I continued to let him lead and leisurely watched while a new battalion of ticks marched up his back.

Two hours into the trail, I told him it was time for an early lunch.

We sat down on a log and leaned back into another that had fallen across it. I unpacked my meal of apples, almonds, oranges, cheese, and strawberries. He pulled out a crumpled, rectangular energy bar from his pocket. Amid much crinkling and the confession that he possessed "gorilla fingers," my student made his way into the silver-lined package.

"Oh good God!" he protested.

After rolling his jaw a few times, he dribbled the chewed portion of the trail snack into his injured palm and tossed the mushy wad in the woods. He quickly followed this with two big gulps of water, which he swished around his mouth and spit out.

"How the hell do you guys eat these . . . these . . . sticks of cardboard?" he inquired as he, elbow locked, held what remained in front of him and, twisting his wrist so he could survey both sides, gave the compressed sheet of lacquered granola a look of disdain. "I paid two bucks for this thing!" he declared.

I didn't answer and waited for him to turn my direction. When he did, I raised my eyebrow, held up an orange slice, and slid it in my mouth.

"Oh," he said, accompanied by an uncharacteristically humble smile.

I walked over to a wild rose and plucked several marble-sized seed pods that looked like miniature pomegranates.

"Here. Try this," I said once I'd squeezed out the arsenic-laden seeds, leaving only the fleshy, pumpkin-orange pulp and maroon rind.

"What's that?" my student asked, his eyes widening as if I were trying to hand him a Democratic ballot.

"Rose hips. Try them. They taste like a cross between an apple and, well, a rose."

"I'm not eating *that*," he barked. "It's been in the dirt."

"Seriously?" I asked, waiting for him to put two and two together. He continued to stare at me blankly.

"You only eat hydroponics?" I asked.

"Hydro what?"

"Ponics. Plants they grow without soil."

"They can do that? Is it expensive?"

"Yes, but ...." I paused a moment to compose myself and redirect the question. "Let me ask you this: You own a restaurant, okay?"

He nodded, indicting he was along for the hypothetical ride. I continued.

"Do you buy the really expensive food for your customers?"

"Not unless that's what they're wanting. That'd be stupid. 'Buy low, sell high.'"

"Alright. You eat out a lot?"

"Yeah. Got to with my job."

"Well then, here's some more."

"Some more what?"

"Dirt food, only this time it's fresh."

After thinking about this a moment, he shrugged, said "Huh, I guess you're right," and reluctantly took what I was offering. He placed a rose hip on the tip of his tongue. Realizing it didn't taste like dirt, he slowly put the fruit in his mouth as he scrutinized my face for the slightest hint of an emerging grin.

"Not bad," he said after chewing it a little. "Kinda has a lemony flavor."

"More vitamin C than an orange," I informed him.

"Really?" he said, surprised. "They're so little," he commented as he looked down at the ones left in his hand before tossing them in his mouth.

Knowing it'd be lost on him, I nonetheless added, "And no one's been out here to douse them with pesticides. Technically, you're eating really expensive organic gourmet food for free."

"Huh," he said insipidly.

"I gotta go pee," I told him, then sauntered off into the woods.

As I tinkled, I thought back over the wild food debate and grimaced when it occurred to me that I hadn't included grocery store produce in my argument. Since my mind was elsewhere, I didn't fully commit to the urination, which forced me to downgrade it to a lackadaisical 3. When I arrived back at the trail, my student was nowhere to be found.

Assuming he'd gone off to relieve himself as well, I returned to my lunch. After several minutes passed, and more curious than concerned, I peered over one shoulder, then the other, on the off chance I'd spot him on his way back. My cursory survey revealing nothing, I tucked an apple slice and two chunks of cheese in my cheeks and shoved a handful of almonds in my pocket, packed up the rest of my food, and made sure I had enough water for both of us. Still not having returned, I began to get worried because I knew he wasn't comfortable enough in the wild to take an extended bathroom break outdoors and seriously doubted he'd had the foresight to stash a few squares of toilet paper in his pocket in case nature called. My mind roamed for a second as I envisioned flop sweat coursing down his forehead as he faced Sophie's Choice: monogrammed handkerchief or sycamore leaf. Snapping out of my comical daydream, I listened once again for movement in the bush. Silence. I took a few steps into the trail so I could see further along its curved path. Nothing. Then I heard it.

"Pssst."

A noise, less like a ticked off critter and more like a leaky pipe.

"Pssssst. Over here."

On the far side of the lower tree trunk that we had been sitting on was the top half of my student's head, his fingers bordering either cheek as they hovered over the edge of the log. I was impressed. He was a very large man and had clearly gone to considerable lengths to contort his body into approximately eight very dense cubic feet of person.

"What are you —?"

"*Look*," he urgently whispered as he poked a finger to my right, "over there."

I glanced in the direction he was pointing. I saw nothing.

"Pssssssssssst."

I turned back.

"Over *there*," he said under his breath with a slight nod of the head, "in that pile of leaves." As if whatever he was afraid of would seek revenge for him having ratted it out, he ducked behind the fallen tree.

I looked again. There was a mound of leaves the wind had gathered at the base of a shagbark hickory. I couldn't see anything on, in, or near them.

"What?" I whispered while asking myself why *I* was whispering.

He poked his head back over the trunk. "Snake," he faintly muttered, so as not to risk alerting it to his presence, before retreating to safety.

"What kind?" As soon as the question escaped my lips, I knew I'd wasted my breath.

"Dunno. The bad kind? I just saw something move all of

a sudden."

I started to walk over.

"No!" he screamed as he catapulted out of his hiding spot. He grabbed my shoulders and pulled me back.

Hardly able to believe his reaction, I turned to face him. He didn't give me a chance to speak.

"No," he pleaded. "It'll eat you," he informed me while peeking over my shoulder at the heap of decaying vegetation. Thinking this was the coup de grâce of a cleverly elaborate joke by a former frat boy, I started to smile, but his quivering chin caught my attention. He was serious.

I rolled my eyes and turned around. Ignoring the fact that I now had a 230-pound man wedged in the small of my back, I left my student to fend for himself and stepped forward to see if I could confirm the sighting. I tried to detect an inconsistency in the leaves' pattern. Finding none, I took a stick and prodded the pile. Nothing moved. Convinced it was a false alarm, I begun kicking the dead foliage to emphasize it was safe.

My student shrieked. I gave him a look of beleaguered condemnation. Once his hyperventilated gasps became faint puppy whimpers, I demanded he come over to where I was standing. Speechless, he stared at me, then at the stack of disheveled leaves, and back at me before frantically shaking his head.

"Get your ass over here," I commanded. "You probably saw a skink moving around. If there'd been a snake, I would have either found it or I've scared it off by now."

I'd spoken before thinking.

Having made him aware the latter was a possibility, he darted quick glances all around and then scampered to the top of the downed tree we'd been using as a backrest. There he stood, all four snake-defying feet in the air, completely petrified, gawking at me.

"Dammit. There's nothing—"

"Take a picture," he insisted as he tossed me his phone.

I had to hand it to him. The way he'd gone about scaling the log, I was sure I was going to have to dial the fire department before nightfall. "The purpose of my call? There's an executive stuck in a tree. Instead of a saucer of milk and 'Here kitty, kitty, kitty,' someone might want to bring a hedge fund and a recording of George Bush promising 'No new taxes.'" But my student had thankfully given me an alternative: He'd agreed to climb down if I produced a non-slithering, non-venomous photograph of rotting plant matter. So I walked over and took a picture.

As I did so, I thought to myself, *Let's have some fun with this!* I stooped over as if something had suddenly caught my eye.

"What is it? What do you see? Is it a snake? How big is it?" a voice murmured above me.

Before I had a chance to respond, it occurred to me that I'd mentally quoted Fraggle Fern. Decidedly mischievous, playful nuances were running through my inherited park chemistry. My good-natured ribbing of the arboreal businessman was eerily reminiscent of the director sending me on a snipe hunt. I'd come full-circle. Like those before me, *I* was now passing along the forest's initiation rites.

"I think . . . . Yep," I said definitively as I pointed at the scattered debris. "There it is."

"What? What is it? Is it poisonous? Will it eat me?"

"The exact place where a snake *wasn't.*"

"Ha ha," he said. "But really," he quickly followed. "Is there a snake?"

I walked over and handed him the phone. He leaned forward, snatched it from my fingers, pulled it close to his face, and inspected the photo. Once his initial evaluation was complete, he started looking back and forth—from the picture to the pile of leaves, from the leaves to the picture—comparing the two.

After much coaxing, he reluctantly made his descent.

When I was sure both his feet were on solid ground, I said, "That was a close one."

He jerked, uncertain whether he should do another frightened squirrel impression. "Those invisible snakes can be vicious," I remarked, while issuing him one of his own patented winks.

He smirked. A tick emerged over the top of his right ear.

"Well, Indiana Jones, you about ready to shove off again?" I asked.

"I guess," he sighed.

Noticing he no longer had it with him and that it wasn't lying anywhere nearby, I asked, "Where's the walking stick?"

"Huh. I dunno," he said with alarm, unaware he was no longer in possession of it. "Guess I tossed it when I took off running. Sorry. Wasn't thinking."

"Took off running? You weren't more than five feet from where we were sitting."

"I know."

"Where's the machete?"

"No clue," he said with a shrug and apologetic smile.

Once we located the machete and thinking it best to only give my student sharp objects under close supervision, I clipped it back on my bag, found another trekking pole, and headed down the trail.

An hour later, we arrived at our destination: the downed tree that had been reported. It was a pignut hickory. I pointed out its cute, snout-nosed seeds which littered the forest floor before freeing the ax from the crosscut's clutches and laying the saw on the trunk. As I looked up at the sky to see if the weather was going to remain steady, I held out the ax and told my student to peel the bark from around the log where the tree met the edge of the trail. After a few moments of holding the tool at arm's length in silence, only to find myself continuing to do so, I glanced over.

Not again, I thought as I propped the ax against the hickory.

The first thing I did was check the other side of the fallen timber by leaning over the trunk. There he was: compact, trembling, and staring into a wall of wood. I half expected him to be sucking his thumb.

"What? Where's the imaginary python this time?" I huffed.

He looked up at me.

"By your foot," he whispered.

I pushed myself off the log and looked down. A small piece of a mature, woody vine that had been growing up the side of the pignut had broken off and landed on the trail. I picked it up.

"This, my friend, is the highly aggressive, very deadly Midwest tree adder," I reported as I draped myself back over the trunk and dangled it in his face. He made a primal yelp and tried scuttling backward, but because he'd been squatting, merely toppled over. Realizing what I had in my hand was only dead foliage, he got up, dusted himself off, and joined me on the other side of the hickory.

"Man, I should have used the bathroom back there," he casually noted in hopes of downplaying his embarrassment. "Where's the closest restroom?" he asked as he scoured the nearby hillsides for an outhouse.

"Gotta go off-trail," I told him while I started unsheathing the crosscut.

"What? Why? Where'd you go when you went back there on the trail?"

"Off-trail."

He peered into the forest.

"Nope. Nuh-uh. No siree. No way. Not gonna happen. There's snakes out there. I'll hold it," he declared.

Having passed the bathroom verdict, he asked, "So, what are we doing today?"

I reached over, picked up the ax, and handed it to him.

"We're taking out this bad boy," I said. "Go strip the bark from around that side of the tree," I instructed as I nodded at the walkway's perimeter.

"Strip the bark?"

"Like a cigar band," I said as I made a loop in the air with my finger. He took the ax and tossed his chin in my direction to indicate he understood the simile.

Happy he was safe and could be contributing, my student set to work. Once I'd finished unbinding the crosscut and retrieved two wedges and the bottle of vegetable oil from my backpack, I checked his progress.

He had taken a wide stance and was trying to shear the tree's skin with swooping, full-bodied, Bunyan-quality swings. I admired him. Although the ax was ricocheting off the log more than it was impacting it, he remained positive. I casually glanced down at his new boots and noticed a beige-and-brown ball almost equidistant from his heels. My eyes widened.

A copperhead.

A real, bonafide, in the flesh, very venomous, cat-eyed copper-head.

Standing at rapt attention.

Animals that blend in with their surroundings — such as copperheads, which are notorious for melting into like-colored leaf litter — are *typically* less likely to attack unless provoked, since doing so would betray their veiled position. The only reason my student hadn't been bitten was that he had yet to brush up against the coiled serpent. All he had to do was adjust his footing and his epic phobia would be justified.

"Hey," I said, as casually as possible, while looking up at him and then down at the snake.

"Yeah?" he replied as he brought the ax up over his head.

"Stop."

Confused and perhaps thinking that he'd done something wrong, he lowered the ax and looked at me. When I didn't meet his gaze, he started to follow my sightline.

"No!" I yelled while darting my hand out in front of me. *"Don't look down and don't move."*

"Ha, ha," he playfully sneered. He widened his stance before tossing the ax back over his head.

"Stop!"

Realizing I was serious, he looked down. Not immediately noticing the snake, he begun to step back.

"Stop!" I roared. He froze and looked up at me, awaiting direction.

I told him where to look and why it was vital for him to stay where he was.

"Wha —, what am I supposed to do?" he cried.

In a calm, soothing voice, I instructed him to move ever so slowly away from the copperhead and under no circumstance make any sharp, abrupt movements. He started to lift his left leg. Time stopped dead because his boot was shaking uncontrollably. His involuntary reflex was probably equal parts fear and sustained, painful muscle constriction since he was trying to hold his leg—which wasn't accustomed to the weight of his new footwear—surgically steady. What seemed like hours later, he set his foot on the ground behind him. He then repeated the slow motion process with his right foot. Afterward, and with the same delicacy, he stepped back a few more times. Now safely out of striking distance, I glanced at his face. He was white as a sheet and on the verge of passing out.

I got out my camera and climbed on top of the log. To keep from spooking the little guy, I eased myself down and hugged the timber so I'd have a better vantage point. As I took pictures, I marveled at the reptile's Zen-like stillness and exquisite coloration. Perhaps sensing the immediate threat had past and bored with the paparazzi, it slithered off into the woods. Overjoyed, I looked up at my student from my prostrate position.

"You okay?" I asked as I spun around and sat up.

"Yeah. I think so," he meekly squeaked. "But I don't need to pee anymore."

He wasn't joking. His right inseam was soaked from crotch to cuff.

I was envious. He'd just achieved the Holy Grail of urinations, a Perfect 10, and didn't even know it.

Barely containing my laughter, I decided the fallen tree could wait another day.

I called my student the following evening to see how he was doing.

"Oh fine. Fine," he said with mocking, faux reassurance. "Could you hold on a sec?" There was a brief pause and then, in the background, the sound of pages being hastily turned. "I want to thank you for letting me go hiking with you yesterday."

"Hey, no—"

"It afforded me the opportunity to get out of the office for a little while. I saw some cool things that I wouldn't have got to see otherwise." I could hear him checking off the items as he went along. "I got to eat some weird shit, and only suffered a minor heart attack in the process." I had no doubt he'd actually written "ate weird shit" in his notes.

"You find any more ticks on you after you got back home?"

"A few. Not that many. In round figures, twenty-eight, not counting the one that was crawling up my neck this morning. I'd taken two showers since then."

"Yeah, they can be a bit clingy."

"The one this morning . . . I hadn't had my coffee yet. Freaked my ass out. I broke a lamp trying to get it off."

"How about the boots? You get a chance to—?"

I was interrupted by an exasperated, prolonged sigh.

"The boots. Let me tell you about the boots. So I walk in and put them on the counter, right? The guy takes the lid off the box to make sure they're alright. Starts flipping them over, looking at the soles. You know, whatever. Then he notices what he called a 'slight discoloration' on the top of the right one. He shows it to me and asks what it is while he's rubbing it, seeing whether he can get it off with his thumb."

"What was it?"

"Well, *I* knew what it was, but he'd put me on the spot all of a sudden. I couldn't come up with anything fast enough, so I told him."

He waited for me to ask again. I just let the suspense build.

"So I told him. 'Pee,' I said. He gives me *this look*, drops the shoe back in the box, pushes them back at me, and says the store has a strict 'No pee' return policy."

A week later I got a letter in the mail. It was from my student. When I opened it, his business card flitted to the floor. He'd also enclosed two tickets to a herpetarium an hour north. When I went to pick the card up off the floor, I noticed there was something written on the back.

Professor,

Enjoy. Take your wife. Tell her it's great and that I went last week for free. Make sure she brings an extra pair of pants.

Afterword

Why Hike?

Someone once told me, "If you can walk, you can hike." That person obviously never tried "hiking" through Maine's famed Mahoosuc Notch along the Appalachian Trail—a mile-long jumble of boulders that forces hikers to become gymnasts in order to make forward progress. There's also 13,200-foot Forester Pass along the Pacific Crest Trail in California. To follow the trail up and over that pass, most early spring hikers have to cross a vertigo-inducing snow chute that will make you struggle to remember the particulars of your life insurance policy. And of course I'd be remiss if I didn't mention the snowmelt-swollen rivers of the Bob Marshall Wilderness along the Continental Divide Trail in Montana. "Hiking" the trail there involves waist-deep double fords that are better suited to river rafting than walking.

Sometimes though, it is just as simple as a walk in the woods. Following a distant path into a darkened forest can be one of the most stress-reducing and physically invigorating efforts you have at your disposal. And the price of admission isn't bad either—many trails are free or a couple of bucks at most. No special skill set is required. Emerson said, "Few people know how to take a walk. The qualifications are endurance, plain clothes, old shoes, an eye for nature, good humor, vast curiosity, good speech, good silence and nothing too much." You don't necessarily have to wear old shoes, but good humor will definitely help, especially when you think you are almost back to the trailhead and realize you've still got a mile to go.

Hiking, of course, is made much easier because of trails. We all owe a debt of gratitude to the folks that build and maintain trails. Trails provide the avenues that allow us to enter the wilderness and ultimately the wilderness's beauty, change of scenery, and lack of clutter are what we are after. Taking a hike allows us to connect with a part of ourselves that we lose to the 40-hour workweek, corner office, rush hour traffic, and the desire to always be plugged in and connected.

A hike in the woods also forces us to relinquish the safety found in the climate-controlled boxes most of us call home. It forces us to make our way in a drastically different environment and to contend with that environment not on our terms, but on hers. If it rains, you put on a rain jacket. If it's too hot, shed a layer. Too cold, add a layer. No thermostat to adjust here—just our attitudes and how we perceive comfort and discomfort. But therein lies the beauty. Being outside on a hike allows us the opportunity to be how we originally were . . . bipedal organisms out and about making our way here and there. It allows us to clear our minds and to hit the reset button. It allows us to get some fresh air and a workout without really feeling like it is exercise. It allows us to *be*.

When the trail becomes steep and jagged, we might find ourselves breaking a sweat. So much the better. Manual labor and physical work can do wonders to rid our minds of the restlessness most of us feel as a result of living urban lives in artificial environments. Initially, the sore muscles and heavy breathing we find as we labor uphill on trail can leave us grumpy and exasperated. Over time though, our bodies adjust and we find that long hike we just completed left us stronger and in search of the next trail. Before you know it, you may find yourself adjusting your schedule, weekend plans, and summer vacation to get your next fix—a hike on that new trail. That feeling of contentedness that washes over you after finishing a hike can be addicting. The cure can only be found on the next trail.

There is something to be said too about the rhythm of nature. For all of us in the Northern Hemisphere, the sun rises in the east, arcs to the south, and sets in the west. Most of us don't have a chance to notice such things from the fluorescently-lit cubicles we go to five days a week to earn a living. Being on-trail gives us front row seats to such spectacles. On longer hikes you may even find yourself waking up at sunrise (without the aid of an alarm clock) and wanting to turn in at sunset. With a lack of artificial lighting at night, it's truly amazing how quickly our bodies "know" when it's time to sleep. And sleep ... that wonderful thing that can elude us while we lay awake at night staring at the ceiling wondering if we hit "send" on that last email, got that report in on time, or are adequately prepared for tomorrow's budget meeting. Sleep comes so much more easily and effortlessly when we've put in a full day hiking and have adequately exhausted ourselves.

With that, I encourage you to push back your desk chair, stand up, and walk outside. Go find the nearest trail you have available and start hiking. Go as long and far as you can. Don't stop until you are thoroughly spent and your mind is clear. Even then you may need to go a little farther. John Muir said, "Thousands of tired, nerve-shaken, over-civilized people are beginning to find out going to the mountains is going home."

Welcome home.

Lawton Grinter
Crested Butte, Colorado
August 2014

Lawton Grinter has completed end-to-end hikes of the Appalachian Trail, Continental Divide Trail, and two passes of the Pacific Crest Trail. In addition to the "Big 3," he has also done the John Muir Trail and Colorado Trail in his 10,000+ miles of long-distance hiking since 1999. He is author of I Hike: Mostly True Stories from 10,000 Miles of Hiking *and filmed, edited, and produced the documentary* The Walkumentary, *which covers his 2006 southbound Continental Divide Trail excursion. He currently lives in Denver, Colorado with his wife and fellow long-distance hiker, Felicia Hermosillo, and their dog, Gimpy.*

Appendix I

Additional Resources on Trail Maintenance

As can be imagined, there are not a lot of books on the ins and outs of trail maintenance, especially texts focusing specifically on a particular aspect of the craft. Although I mention Robert Birkby's *Lightly on the Land*—which has since moved into a second, 340-page edition—it is a very basic guide which serves more as an encyclopedia than a comprehensive how-to model. In my humble opinion, the bible of trail maintenance has yet to be written and, to do the trade justice, would have to be several volumes. (For example, the wonderful book you have just finished didn't give me license to discuss many of the nuances of the field, i.e., sterilizing one's lopper blades between snips to inhibit cross-contaminating infection; what to look for in, and how to take care of, a good hiking boot; making sure the cuts made to discarded, severed limbs face *away* from the trail so as not to disrupt nature's meticulous attention to exterior design, etc.)

In its place, there are books largely devoted to trail design and construction, such as *Appalachian Trail Design, Construction, and Maintenance* by William Birchard, and those dealing with region- and traveler-specific trail work, such as Robert Steinholtz's *Wetland Trail Design and Construction* and the IMBA's *Trail Solutions,* respectively. The diversity and complexity can be daunting. Whereas in the Pacific Northwest trail crews have to set up pulleys to move boulders, the team may not be as well versed in puncheon construction as a person responsible for the numerous walkways found in a boggy Florida state park. I have never had to deal with a ski route, but contend with equine trails on a weekly basis, something a park employee addressing mountain bike concerns may never have to worry about. It follows that there are as many maintenance techniques as there are parks. However, ax to my head, if I had to give a thumbs-up to one general, introductory text, though the *Complete Guide to Trail Building and Maintenance* by the Appalachian Mountain Club is nice, it is largely written from an administrative perspective. At the end of the day, I'd offer to those humoring a career in the field Carl Demrow's *Complete Guide to Trail Building and Maintenance*.

As I've stated, a lot of time and sweat will be saved if a person working in the forest knows what type of tree is gracing one's path. A good state-specific book on tree identification is a must. Pray the tree you're working on isn't standing in a tract of poison ivy. Or hiding a copperhead.

Also for trail novices, investing in and memorizing a backpacking guide is priceless. However, although it might seem logical to start with a book written by a veteran hiker, such as someone who has traversed the entire Pacific Crest Trail, it would be a rookie mistake. Endurance and thru hikers have a different priority on the trail, typically speed, which is diametrically opposed to the maintenance worker's agenda, which is strength and balance. For example, a thru hiker might advocate ultralite tennis shoes, but with razor-sharp equipment, a maintenance worker needs stability and protection, so boots are a must. On the other hand, understanding weight distribution in respect to one's backpack is vital (hint: unlike a grocery bag, heavy stuff doesn't go on the bottom), and the same principles apply to hiker and maintenance worker alike. Chris Townsend's *The Backpacker's Handbook* does a good job outlining such concepts and *The Complete Walker* by Colin Fletcher and Chip Rawlins isn't too shabby in this regard either.

The other "must have" is more of a "must do." I strongly suggest taking a first aid class before setting out in the woods on a daily basis. Take my hard-won advice, getting hurt several miles into the wilderness is not fun and help may be many, many hours away, especially if there isn't cell reception. Always tell someone what trail you will be trekking with an anticipated arrival time so they know when it's safe to start divvying up your personal possessions.

That said, don't show up the first day not knowing the behavioral proclivities of your coworkers, i.e., the organisms you will be working around. Watching nature documentaries and reading about the animals that will be sharing the forest with you will cut back on the unpleasant, bladder-voiding surprises. Naturalist David Attenborough has been producing and narrating BBC nature programs for over 30 years. They are as well paced, informative, and entertaining as Marty Stouffer's *Wild America* series, which aired on PBS from 1982 to 1994. These shows are visual starting points and complements to Bernd Heinrich's non-technical, bookend masterpieces on animal behavior, *Winter World* and *Summer World*.

Regarding gear, I believe in the tried-and-true method of trial and error, largely because everyone's needs and tastes differ. Although online reviews and hiking forums are helpful, only you can decide what works best in the woods. Much to my peers' chagrin, my first pair of hiking boots only cost 20 dollars. At the risk of creating trail legend, they lasted for five years. However, one thing I would never skimp on is my ax. Every maintenance worker should be required to test out of Dudley Cook's *The Ax Book*, which ought to have been titled *The Ax Bible* and its design editor was prophetic by setting the type in dual columns. Once a person understands the intricacies of this deceptively simple tool, the individual will spare no expense in dolling out the cash to get a good one. Mine cost 150 bucks and I don't regret having spent a single cent.

It would be silly to hand over half a week's trail maintenance pay on an ax if you don't know how to maintain it. All that needs to be said about John Juranitch's *The Razor Edge Book of Sharpening* is its cover is graced by a picture of the author shaving his face with an ax. If nothing else, he'll convince you a grind stone is worth its weight in gold.

As for crosscut saws, there is a sad literary deficiency in respect to this legendary tool. I strongly advise joining the oral heritage as soon as possible and enrolling in a crosscut workshop while there are still people who know something about the subject. When it comes to picking one out, the old saying "They don't make 'em like they used to" holds true. For example, though the kerf's girth is dependent upon how wide the teeth are set, they can only extend so far before being prone to breakage. It has been many, many decades since a saw manufacturer invested the time and money to cast a blade which is broader at the bottom than at the top of the spine, therefore making the kerf inherently wider and the saw slower to pinch. As such, not only will it be cheaper, but worth the time and effort to find and reinstate a retired, well-engineered crosscut from an antique store. Be sure to give your saw a trail name.

Appendix II

Additional Resources on Wilderness Survival

I continued my wilderness survival education and ultimately wound up teaching introductory courses to both children and adults for several years. There are many facets to this field of anthropological study (shelter, firecraft, water procurement and purification, tools, cordage, flintknapping, knots, tracking/ stalking/hunting, food preparation and storage, and navigation and orienteering). However, unlike most other academic disciplines, wilderness survival is best presented through the visual realm, preferably by a teacher. Hard copy research can then be better understood and will complement hands-on practice.

Although Ray Mears pioneered the genre of televised outdoor skills broadcasting in the late 1990s, wilderness survival didn't become a household name until CBS debuted the reality program *Survivor* in 2000. Albeit entertaining, its Achilles' heel is that, as a season wears on, the producers make survival *easier* on contestants, thereby making them *less* reliant upon primitive methods. The show's popularity spawned an interest in overt survival skills and manifested in the premier of two related, multi-season instructional documentaries, *Survivorman* in 2004 and *Man vs. Wild* in 2006. The latter harbors much controversy in that many survival experts doubt the authenticity of the program's contents, and its host, Bear Grylls, promotes a multitude of survival tactics which are considered dubious at best and dangerous at worst. After this time, numerous other television shows appeared, offering much the same as their predecessors. The two I professionally advocate aside from *Survivorman* are Discovery's *I, Caveman* and *Out of the Wild*, especially the Venezuela expedition.

Because the various television programs initiated a wilderness survival craze, a barrage of texts soon hit the market. However, very little new information was presented that improved upon the time-tested books which were already available. As I have previously noted, Tom Brown's *Field Guide to Wilderness Survival* is worth rebuying after you drop your first copy in a puddle. However, this is only an introductory guide to the multi-faceted world of how primitive man lived on a daily basis.

In respect to shelter construction, D.C. Beard's *Shelters, Shacks, and Shanties* is a solid effort. When it comes to navigation, Harold Gatty never loses his reader in *Finding Your Way Without Map or Compass*. As far as primitive tools and weaponry go, Jim Hamm's *Bows & Arrows of the Native Americans* hits the mark, and John Whittaker's *Flintknapping* is hard to beat. It is also worth hunting down Paul Rezendes' *Tracking and the Art of Seeing* and, justifiably so, many people swear by Dale Martin's *The Trapper's Bible*.

Although generalized texts discussing plants and ethnobotany are ill-advised and should be replaced with regional books written by area scholars, Thomas Elias' *Edible Wild Plants*, Samuel Thayer's *The Forager's Harvest*, and Steven Foster's *A Field Gide to Medicinal Plants and Herbs* are dependable references. However, I would <u>never</u> recommend self-instruction in this subfield, which <u>should only be undertaken with the guidance and supervision of a trained professional</u>. There is little glory to be had in your loved ones telling former coworkers that you died after nibbling on death camas because you thought it was wild onion.

Only after an individual has attempted to implement and utilize one's wilderness survival training will the person come to appreciate Mario Bigon's *The Morrow Guide to Knots*.

For the casual armchair adventurer who has no interest in getting dirty but wants an entertaining as well as educational peek into the past, Jean Auel's *Earth's Children* series, beginning with her most famous work, *The Clan of the Cave Bear*, is acclaimed for its comprehensiveness and accuracy in depicting primitive man's daily existence. The non-fiction companions to Auel are Irven Devore and Richard Lee's *Man the Hunter* and Marshall Shalins' *Stone Age Economics*. However, reader beware: The latter two texts are in-depth anthropological studies of primitive man, meaning they are rewarding, but rather sterile, reading. To counter this (and its goes without saying), the most famous fictional tale of modern survival is Daniel Defoe's *Robinson Crusoe*. Beginning survival students are often surprised at how plausibly the titular character's trials and tribulations are depicted. This is because they are based on real-life castaway Alexander Selkirk, whose biography, *Selkirk's Island* by Diana Souhami, is worth checking out for this reason. Finally, the cinematic equivalent to Defoe's novel is Robert Zemeckis' Oscar-nominated film *Cast Away*, starring Tom Hanks.

Without reservation, I recommend these items before any how-to manual because they convey the most important skills necessary for surviving in the wild: psychological fortitude and emotional stability.

Appendix III

A Very Annotated Reading List
on Nature Writing

Admittedly, my worldview has been influenced by nature writers, namely Thoreau, but as any wilderness author will tell you, a book about nature is—like porn is to sex—a poor substitute for the real thing. Regardless of how skilled a wordsmith may be, the thrill of *not* seeing one's first tree snorer cannot be captured on the written page. That said, the genre of nature writing is as diverse as the wilds themselves. Should you have found my bibliographical suggestions interesting, here's a list of kindred spirits.

The best literary sampling for someone who wants to dip their toes in the ocean of nature literature before diving into a book-length pond is Library of America's doorstop anthology, *American Earth: Environmental Writing Since Thoreau*. Even as a former literature professor, this patchwork of excerpts is one of my desert island picks. The only things missing are selections from two National Book Award winners: *Arctic Dreams* by Barry Lopez and Peter Matthiessen's *The Snow Leopard*.

John McPhee's prose is as eloquent as it is insightful. Through the mere power of a carefully-crafted sentence, he brings a novel-quality allure to nature and the people within it.

Although I only had occasion to make passing reference to him, Edward Abbey delivers humor and unapologetic social criticism to a typically stuffy genre. But proceed with caution: His non-fiction is much more controlled and focused than his novels.

For fear of someone claiming I overlooked a master, I will pause to say I'm not a huge fan of John Muir for the reasons I outline when discussing Dillard. He is more of a biologist's nature writer than an armchair adventurer or literary reader's author.

In respect to fiction, the genre of eco-criticism is taking off. The analytic technique examines ecological themes in novels, short stories, plays, and poetry. Nature has been represented on the written page since the Greeks, but it did not become a preoccupation until modern society had largely separated itself from the environment. Once this occurred, authors began to idolize, and subsequently idealized, what they could only fathom in the abstract. It is easy to pinpoint when this first took place and serves to illustrate how literature is partner to history: A surge of such ideas appears in the work of the Romantic poets. Although there are a few exceptions, American writers had to wait until a century later, after the frontier was conquered, before they realized, and started to lament with their pens, what they too had lost. Eco-criticism's current fixation is the American pastoral tradition in 20th-century fiction.

Thomas Hardy is the forefather of the environmental novel and his dark but honest parables are a staple in the field. *The Return of the Native* is his most recognizable in this regard, yet I prefer *The Woodlanders*. Even though Rachel Carson complained about this half a century ago, the ecological insight offered by the maritime narrative is still being overlooked. Perhaps somewhat predictably, I enjoy the understated humor in Herman Melville's *Moby Dick* (the author's research was so thorough and groundbreaking, one edition of the epic omitted the main storyline entirely, leaving only the chapters dealing with cetology—the study of whales). Another, criminally ignored, eco favorite is James Dickey's cautionary fable, *Deliverance*. As far as contemporary literature goes, Barbara Kingsolver brings a refreshing female perspective to the male-dominated arena and is the strongest voice in environmental fiction today.

Science fiction also tows its fair share of the ecological line, beginning with cornerstones such as J.G. Ballard's *World* quadrilogy, Frank Herbert's *Dune*, and John Brunner's *The Sheep Look Up*. Margaret Atwood and Kim Stanley Robinson are proudly carrying on this tradition, the former giving audiences post-apocalyptic nightmares with her *MaddAddam* series while the latter anticipates the dilemmas involved in the terraformation of other planets (which is a wry, roundabout way of commenting on what we are doing to the Earth) in his *Mars* trilogy. An eco sci-fi up-and-comer is Paolo Bacigalupi. Although derivative of Brunner, he reminds us that things aren't getting any better in *The Windup Girl*. And finally, because it deserves a second mention, I cannot say enough about George Stewart's biologically- and anthropologically-astute *Earth Abides*.

I would rather be ashes than dust!

I would rather that my spark should burn out in a brilliant blaze than it should be stifled by dry-rot.

I would rather be a superb meteor, every atom of me in magnificent glow, than a sleepy and permanent planet.

The function of man is to live, not to exist.

I shall not waste my days in trying to prolong them.

I shall use my time.

Attributed to Jack London

Michael Gurnow is author of the bestselling *The Edward Snowden Affair: Exposing the Politics and Media Behind the NSA Scandal*. His writing has been selected as Editor's Choice, served as cover stories, included in college curriculums, and cited in newspapers and literary and law journals. A former English professor, he is currently trail maintenance coordinator at one of the most popular state parks in America. He lives on an organic farm with his very hippie wife.